Navigating International Business and Entering New Markets

Robert S. Pearlstein and Janet A. Gregory

Printed by CreateSpace Independent Publishing
North Charleston, SC

www.createspace.com

ISBN-13: 9781545146668
ISBN-10: 1545146667

Library of Congress Control Number: 2017905582
CreateSpace Independent Publishing Platform
North Charleston, South Carolina

To

William W. Wilmot

For his wisdom, inspiration,
first outline, and encouragement

Contents

Acknowledgments

Ed Gregory—encouragement & patience
Sharon Pearlstein—encouragement & patience

Influential books (more listed in resources & references)

* Curtis Carlson and William Wilmot, *Innovation: The Five Disciplines for Creating What Customers Want*
* James Foley, *The Global Entrepreneur*
* Frank Lavin and Peter Cohan, *Export Now*
* Mona Pearl, *Grow Globally: Opportunities for Your Middle-Market Company around the World*
* John Warrillow, *Built to Sell*

Curt Carlson, author of *Innovation*—advice on the big ideas
Mike Gospe, author of *Marketing Campaign Development, The Marketing High Ground*, and *The Flip Chart Guide to Customer Advisory Boards*—getting started & ongoing guidance
Kathy Hullman, author of *Starting up Silicon Valley*—publishing realities

Kimberly Benson—international distribution insights
Andrew Cadwell—entering new markets and international expansion insights
Susan Castoro—graphic advice
Jik Chu—understanding mountain guides and international expansion
Janice Hulse—peer review and international experience insights
Kevin McCoy—international expansion insights
Daniel Turner—international experience insights

Felipe Aceituno—peer review
Grzegorz Albrecht—peer review
William Beuck—buyer perception
Scott Bramwell—photography
David Brockington—peer review
Lainee Goldman—icon artwork
Judy Hewitt—copy and line editing
Maurice Kogen—international trade insights
Beau Peters—peer review
Jorja Rule—copy, line, and content editing
Matt Tankersley—peer review
Susie Williams—image format assistance

Chapter 1

Going Global

He didn't want to be chosen. Frankly, he didn't really know how it happened, but it did. Was this a test? It could be tricky, and yet it was exciting.

Each year TolpaTek[1] *develops a detailed annual plan and three-year outlook. The business plan always includes one or two new challenges or stretch goals—growth, talent, R&D, new markets, product launch, profitability, or just about anything. This year's challenge is to take the company into international markets.*

TolpaTek has built a strong customer base with good consistent growth. The company does business across the United States and in several Canadian provinces, and it even has a few customers in other countries. US expansion has been relatively easy for TolpaTek, entering new regional markets and expanding into new industries. The company holds a strong competitive position and solid market share but is always looking to improve. Steve and Alex, the CEO and executive vice president, respectively, feel confident in the company's ability to meet and exceed expectations.

International markets offer growth and upside potential for TolpaTek. It has had some success in Canada, but outside of North America, the road to business growth has been bumpy.

The planning process is spread over several months to minimize business interruption and allow time for the executive team to investigate new ideas. The entire executive team is involved in the planning process: engineering, marketing, human resources, production, sales, and finance.

The executive team embraces the new international outlook with interest. Yes, TolpaTek has done business outside the United States, but not with any real focus or goals. Now the team is talking about becoming a global company!

At the end of one off-site planning session, other executives slap Alex on the back, and comments run the gamut from enthusiasm to humor to fear. "You've got the company on a global growth trajectory!" "Will you still talk with us lowly office workers once you're a globe-trotter?" "This international diversion will take valuable resources away from our core business."

One message is clear to Alex: "Tag. You're it." The primary responsibly has fallen on his shoulders to successfully take the company into international markets. This is exciting but also daunting. Alex's career has been primarily focused on US business, and his first question echoes: "Where do I start?"

New Reality of Business

By 2020 it is estimated that 95 percent of the world's middle-class consumers will be residing outside US borders.[2] It is clear that the future of the US economy is going to depend upon embracing a global strategy. More important than the sheer size of the numbers, there have been three major factors that have accelerated the pace of global economic change in recent years. The three major factors, identified by Lavin and Cohan in *Export Now,*[3] are the following:

1) Three billion new global customers
2) The death of distance
3) The reduction of trade barriers

If that is not enough, here are some startling facts about the shift in global population by 2050 according to the Pew Research Center (www.pewresearch.org):

* The world's population is forecasted to rise to 9.3 billion.
* India and China (the first and second largest countries by population in 2050) will together hold about one-third of the global population.
* Nigeria will displace the United States as the world's third-largest country by population.

Success in new foreign markets is difficult.

After working for a series of high-technology companies in Silicon Valley, California, over the last twenty-plus years, we found that many companies are strong in innovation and entrepreneurship, yet they remain weak in their ability to internationalize and successfully open up new foreign markets. Accessing new international markets is often an afterthought or a hasty reactive decision, rather than a proactive, thoughtful, ongoing strategic process.

Why don't more companies take a proactive approach to international business?

For the last fifty years, the US economy has been growing steadily. Even with economic fluctuations, the United States remains one of the biggest markets in the world. Entering an overseas market can be hard and risky. Obviously, it is easier to do business in a place where the culture, customs, language, laws, and currency are the same. Many companies will successfully survive and even thrive by simply mining the US market. That's okay—if you want to remain a small- to medium-sized business.

The world has changed.

Wake up to the new reality of business. For long-term success, you must take your business outside of the United States. We live in a global economy. The new reality of business is that you cannot rely on economic growth within the United States alone. The US economy isn't the only market with opportunity. The US economy just isn't growing very fast. Yes, the US economy is still big—one of the biggest in the world. It's a great place to launch and initiate your value proposition. The US market is your proving ground.

The time when we could solely rely on the size and rapid growth of the US economy to help our business survive and prosper is gone. *Gone.*

What is different today as opposed to in the past?

Lavin and Cohan tell us it's three major factors.

> The emergence of **three billion new customers** reflects the transformation of the world economy brought about over the past three decades, as China, and now India, move to market economies with a growing middle class. Consistent with this trend, and somewhat prompted by it, markets have been rationalized. Countries not previously seen as part of the world economy are now being integrated into it, such as countries in Latin America, Central Europe, and the former Soviet Union. The result is that the economic population of the planet has effectively doubled in one generation.
>
> **The death of distance** refers to the rapid decline of geography as a business constraint. Goods, people, and ideas move around the world rapidly and inexpensively. Business activities that once had to

be undertaken at one locale can now be disaggregated and spread around the world. The advent of the Internet, mobile phones, and webcams has led to a collapse in the cost of communication. The emergence of global express delivery, integrated logistics, containerized shipping, and discount air travel has led to a sharp reduction in transportation costs. Goods and ideas move around the world cheaper and faster than at any time in history.

The third major factor is the continued **reduction of trade barriers** by GATT (General Agreement on Tariffs and Trade), WTO (World Trade Organization), and in-country conditions; there are over six hundred free-trade agreements currently in place. It is easier to do business in another country and to work with different currencies.

Why should you care?

Foreign markets are growing, developing, and showing great potential. More importantly, your competition is not sitting on its laurels. Perhaps US companies should be less concerned about global competition from China, Brazil, and India than about companies coming out of other places like Singapore, Israel, Finland, and Chile. These smaller countries are aggressively looking outside their home markets. Smaller countries look beyond their borders for expansion; they are hungry, super competitive, and investing heavily to succeed on the global economic stage. It is almost as easy for a company in Finland to go after the US market as it is for them to go into neighboring countries such as Sweden or Denmark.

In many ways it is a requirement for US companies to consider international and global markets when starting a business or launching a new product. Not having aspirations to address markets outside the country is short-sighted and potentially risky. If you're in any sector of the tech business—biotech, clean tech, or high tech—know that your competitors are investing in global markets.

Why Read *Built for Global*?

If United States–based companies are to flourish, the business perspective needs to be global. Our business perspective must extend beyond simple revenue and profit goals, by making a commitment to **establish global-minded operating principles**.

US companies need to be on the offensive and enter new international markets. The goal of *Built for Global* is to provide you with the essential operating principles for navigating international business and entering new markets.

Built for Global provides well-practiced tools and methodology needed to compete and win in new markets. The book is designed to help you, the leader of a small- to medium-sized enterprise (SME), or a division leader within a larger enterprise, enter foreign markets and generate meaningful sales growth. *Built for Global* will teach you

- ✓ the art of communicating value with purpose,
- ✓ the best way to take calculated risks in small steps,
- ✓ how to tap in-country networks with a mountain guide, and
- ✓ methods for building a climate of trust.

Built for Global helps you build global-minded operating principles and opens a fast track to success with an exceptional value proposition. Remove or reduce risks that could be speed bumps or barriers. Accelerate market entry with a great team at home and in-country.

Built for Global gives you the tools to assess your ability to succeed. At the end of key chapters, you will find a self-assessment where you can rate yourself. You will identify weak areas that require attention and strengths worthy of investment. Give these assessments to others in your company to provide you with additional insight, a more complete perspective, and fuel for some great conversations!

Built for Global helps you 1) select the right market, 2) identify the right market timing that best aligns your offering to market need, 3) prepare to make the right investment by reducing speculation and understanding potential risks, 4) leverage the knowledge of your mountain guide for the best market segments, and finally, 5) select the right course of action with the right team.

Anyone can go global—the hard part is to do it profitably with high standards. *Built for Global* is your handbook to essentials of international business. It will show you how to establish value, minimize risk, find guidance, and build trust in foreign markets as you go about scouting, qualifying, and capturing customers in a new country.

Global-minded operating principles will assist you and your business in developing a greater understanding of foreign counterparts. This understanding creates a mutual interdependence that helps you reach the ultimate goals: higher market penetration, revenue, and profits.

The International Expansion Paradox

There is a paradox that firms must grapple with as they embark on international expansion: blind success. It is quite common for a company to achieve a high degree of success in its home market without fully understanding why; that is blind success. Many fine companies have successfully grown at home by mastering a set of activities designed to sell a certain set of products. The result is organic growth: building out production, sales, and a business reputation over the years. Sadly, this often does not translate when expanding into new markets.

To ensure success when entering a new market, a company must expand strategically. You will not have the luxury of organic growth, tackling problems step-by-step over time; you will be forced to address issues in larger increments. With the help of *Built for Global*, you can avoid the trap of blind success leading to blind failure. *Built for Global* addresses four important questions about your company's decision to expand into a new country:

1. **Value.** If it doesn't add value, it's not worth doing. Will your company and product offering succeed in the new country? What value do you bring to customers and to the new market? Will in-country customers buy from you? Can your products and services connect within the new country in a meaningful way? What's the value for your company? Does opening a new international market benefit your company, beyond revenue and profits? We will address these and many other questions in chapter 2, "Add Value."

2. **Risk.** Every new venture involves risk. How can you reduce risk for your company when entering a new international market? What key considerations should you evaluate? Which factors will most likely help or hinder your success? At some point you will need to make that all important "go / no-go" decision. Is there risk for customers in the new country you are entering? Does your offering align with in-country business practices and cultures? We will help you identify and address areas for risk reduction in chapter 3, "De-Risk," and additional considerations in chapter 6, "Are You Going Global?"

3. **Guidance.** Every successful mountain climber knows that, when climbing a challenging and unfamiliar mountain, it is vital to find a *mountain guide* that knows the terrain. When you are entering a new and unfamiliar country, we recommend finding an in-country representative that will be *your* mountain guide. A mountain guide makes connections and establishes confidence in-country, opening doors and building relationships. How do you find a mountain guide? What is the best way to work with a mountain guide? We introduce you to different types of mountain guides and the best practices for working together in chapter 4, "Find a Mountain Guide."

4. **Trust**. A relationship cannot thrive without trust, whether in business or in your personal life. Do you have the support and trust of your company to enter this new market? Internal company resources will be aligned to either work with you…or against you. What is your

proof-of-concept strategy to establish trust with potential customers? We demystify the important elements for building trust with your colleagues at home and your new customers abroad in chapter 5, "Build Trust."

Entering a new international market will take longer than you expect. In the United States today, business is very results oriented. Building value and trust in a new country does not happen overnight; it will take time and may take years. With a mountain guide, you will be able to make short-term progress and see results, but real success is the result of long-term investment. Set expectations that this will take time. Celebrate every little achievement. Your commitment needs to be long-term.

Speed Bumps, Barriers, and Accelerators

As you identify factors that affect your decision to enter into a new market, think about the role of each factor. These will fall into one of three categories: a speed bump, a barrier, or an accelerator. Some factors can fall into more than one category or can change over time. But don't be wishy-washy: identify the primary impact so that you can establish the best strategy to work with it.

If you don't identify the impact a factor can have on your market entry, you won't have an action plan to address it. You want to capitalize on opportunities and minimize the impact of threats.

Speed bumps on a road are designed to reduce speed. When you see this icon of a road with three speed bumps, it will point to things that can slow down your country entry. These are elements to be aware of and to plan for so that you can navigate through and around them. Speed bumps are mostly neutral factors but still require time and energy to understand as you are bringing your product offering into a new country. Cultural considerations and business practices are common examples of speed bumps. In chapter 4, “Find a Mountain Guide,” we will show you how to smooth out potential speed bumps by finding a mountain guide, which can potentially transform into a powerful accelerator. In chapter 5, “Build Trust,” we provide suggestions for transforming home-team and early customer speed bumps into accelerators.

Barriers block or impede progress. Look for this icon of a roadway barricade pointing to issues that can stop your entry into a country or create significant delays if not appropriately addressed. It’s important to identify these elements and establish a plan to minimize or eliminate them. These are negative factors that require investment of time and energy to tackle and resolve. Regulatory requirements, legal prerequisites, and political instability are common examples of barriers. In chapter 3, “De-Risk,” we help you sort out some of the barriers to look for and how to navigate around them.

Accelerators help propel your business in-country. Throughout the book you will see this icon of a rocket ship to indicate opportunities that you want to leverage and capitalize on. Accelerators speed up your progress, provide shortcuts, and reduce barriers. These are positive elements that work with you and provide stimulus and assistance if you appropriately identify them. Invest time and energy to make the most of their influence.

Economic and market trends can be wonderful accelerators with the right business timing. Government initiatives in-country can fast-track progress. In chapter 2, “Add Value,” we help you identify and align your product offering with accelerators.

Don't Let FUD Get in Your Way

Many companies will sooner or later ask themselves, "Should we go international?" In California's Silicon Valley, where Robert and Janet reside, it is top of mind for businesses of every size, from start-up to large enterprise, at every stage of maturity and in every industry. Every business conversation inevitably has a global dimension: international opportunities, world economic issues, global industry trends, and transnational issues.

Global enthusiasm and optimism is often followed by international FUD (fear, uncertainty, and doubt).

Fear of Failure

"What if we fail? If things don't go well, it could have a long-term negative impact on our brand." Chapter 2, "Add Value," and chapter 4, "Find a Mountain Guide," tackle fear of failure head on. If you deliver exceptional value and build trust with a capable mountain guide, you can minimize or eliminate the possibility of failure.

It Costs Too Much

"We don't have the money." "It will distract company resources." "Price and profit pressures are problematic." The willingness to invest time and resources is important to success in any new venture. To maximize the return on investment, it's important to identify and reduce risks, topics that are addressed in chapter 3, "De-Risk."

Fear of Change

"Business is good in the United States." "Our employees (or customers) are comfortable with our business model." "Change is difficult." Venturing into the unknown can be scary without the right skills and good teamwork. Chapter 5, "Build Trust," concentrates on building a winning combination of skills and teamwork at home, in-country, and with customers.

Maybe Later
"The timing is not right." "We are seriously thinking about it (*but not doing anything*)." "We will explore it in a few years." With exceptional value, contained risk, a skilled mountain guide, and a trusted home team, you will wonder why you hadn't ventured into new international markets sooner!

Replace FUD with the four Cs: Communication, Consensus, Collaboration, and Clarity in order to achieve three more Cs: calm, confident conviction. With the help of *Built for Global,* you *can* be successful in new international markets.

The business model detailed in *Built for Global* starts from a position of strength: build a strong value proposition, de-risk with a firm understanding of impact factors in this new market, find a knowledgeable mountain guide, and trust in the strength of your team.

Robert and Janet's Accident with Reality

How does a kid growing up in the streets of Queens, New York, qualify to get involved in international business? We are talking about someone who had never even been on an airplane until he was nineteen years old.

Hello! This is Robert. My accident with the global reality of business started as a skinny kid living in the global village of Jamaica Queens, New York. My dad and mom were both hardworking New Yorkers. My grandparents are from the region known today as the Republic of Belarus. Dad and Mom were born in America, so they are first-generation Americans. Me, I think of myself as just American.

Growing up in Queens was like living in a foreign country. Queens is one of the most ethnically diverse urban areas in the world; 48 percent of the residents of Queens are foreign-born, representing more than one hundred nations and speaking more than 130 languages.[4] *As far as I was concerned, these were my friends, buddies, and playground competitors. I learned that,* ***with a team of diverse skills and capabilities, anything is possible****.*

When I graduated from college, I wasn't exactly sure what I wanted to do or in which direction I should head. I attended a trade show held by Japanese recruitment companies and managed to land a job, even though my Japanese was not very good. Not realizing it, I had already learned the Japanese cultural concept of "gambarimasu," *which essentially means* ***to try, to make your best effort, and to not give up****.*

I lived and worked in Japan for three and a half years before returning to the United States to complete my MBA and to find work. I landed a job with a venture-funded start-up that was positioning itself in one of the business megatrends of the time. ***Participating in a megatrend is both exciting and risky, but it can radically increase the velocity of your business.*** *We took this start-up international at a very early stage, and I helped establish distribution overseas.*

Thus began my serial accidents with the global reality of international business. Next stop...a Silicon Valley, California, start-up. I joined as senior manager of channel development, which was where Janet and I met. This company was very reactionary; it didn't seem to have a plan. There were so many inquiries, and calls came from everywhere. I was jumping on planes chasing anything and everything outside the United States. Chapter 3, "De-Risk," addresses the importance of researching and validating your strategic entry into international markets.

Each successive job had an international component, and I established a track record of helping US companies enter international markets on five continents and more than two dozen countries.

Robert has taken five companies into international markets. They're an interesting mix of public, private, and nonprofit companies that range in size and maturity from large public enterprises to early-stage start-ups. Today Robert is vice president of business development for global partnerships in a large nonprofit research-and-development firm.

How does a kid playing cornfield games in the Midwest end up taking two companies international? This is Janet Gregory's story.

Hi! This is Janet, and my introduction to global business was an accident. Maybe this is a better way to put it: I was hit in the head with it, not once, but multiple times. My concentration was on building expertise in US business development. The United States has markets within markets, and I found the nuances of penetrating these different markets immensely interesting. There is so much opportunity here in the United States that I didn't see the need to look outside of our borders. BONK. It took getting hit in the head with international opportunities to make me see the global reality of business.

I was born and raised in small-town Illinois, northwest of Chicago. My childhood was an uneventful Midwestern upbringing. Midway through high school, Dad's job moved the family to Washington, DC, throwing me into the melting pot of the nation's capital.

*After college I moved west, planting roots in the heart of the Silicon Valley in Northern California. I launched my tech career in customer-facing roles of sales, marketing, and customer service. I learned that **bringing value into any endeavor escalates its chance of success**.*

*Two successful companies led me to a big adventure—my first start-up! I was vice president of sales by title, and typical of a start-up, I was a combination sales manager, sales representative, sales operations, and sales training, all rolled into one. I learned that **the first pilot customers are more precious than gold**. The first customers validated our vision, tested our business model, pricing, and value proposition. In chapter 5, "Build Trust," we talk about the importance of capturing your first customers and establishing a beachhead.*[5]

BONK. International opportunity again hit me on the head. My focus had been entirely US-centric: building a big and profitable domestic business. We were selling to large multinational and global corporations, and our customers wanted systems in Europe and Asia. BONK. BONK. ***Our customers introduced us to partners they trusted, which extended trust in all directions.***

My next start-up was more of a turnaround or a restart. Market timing was right, and we got this company on a fast track to success. BONK. International opportunity hit me in the head again. At least this time, I recognized what was happening. Inquiries started rolling in from around the globe. This evolved into cofounding a consulting firm. It is this work that continues to quench my thirst to connect companies with new customers and new markets.

Janet took three companies into international markets before starting her consulting firm. She now works exclusively to assist companies entering new markets and strategic global expansion.

Self-Assessment: Connect the Dots

Built for Global is meant to be a practical and helpful guide. We know that your business is unique, so at the conclusion of key chapters, we provide the opportunity for you to apply key concepts to your unique business situation. This will help you sort out the most important concepts and develop priorities for your business attention. It is a self-assessment that allows you to analyze where you are in your quest for entering that new market.

In this first self-assessment, connect the dots. You are reading this because you are taking your business international and entering new markets. Connect the dots to what launched this venture. Connect the dots to resources that are readily available to you. Connect with your own international roots.

A Story over Coffee with Daniel Turner
Daniel Turner's personal background plays a key role in his international business success. He very effectively connects the dots with his international roots and leverages them to resolve the many challenges that international business offers.

Daniel was "born on the road," in South Africa, to Canadian diplomatic parents serving overseas. By the time Daniel completed his university education, he had already lived in eleven different countries—and had visited countless more.

During his formative years, Daniel learned the power of what he calls "survival language"—an ability to speak English in varying, yet respectful ways. He could change pace, inflection, vocabulary, and accent so as to be more easily understood. This is an asset that serves him well in all aspects of his extensive career in international business.

In chapter 5, "Build Trust", you will hear Daniel Turner's story of multicultural clashes and cooperation.

① Connect the dots to the **need to take this business international**. Be clear about what is motivating your company to go global.

* What precipitated the effort? Did it start with an internal focus to expand into international markets? Or did it start from external inquiries coming to you?
* What countries outside the United States are you already doing business in?
* What countries are you targeting and why? Be specific about each one.

② Connect the dots to **available expertise**. There are lots of resources available to help you, both formal and informal.

- What expertise within your company are you able to tap into?
  - Which members of the board of directors have contacts that can assist you?
  - Are any current employees from the country (or countries) that you are targeting?

- What expertise outside your company is accessible to you?
  - Who in your business network is doing business in this country today or has done business in this country before? Call them up. Take them out for coffee.
  - What relevant international organizations or associations are available that you might join?

③ Connect the dots to your own **international roots**. This may seem rather basic, but it's important to tap into your own psyche and history. More importantly, it will supply a few fun stories when you are networking!

- What is your ethnic background? Except for Native Americans, everyone came to the United States from somewhere else.
- Did you have a variety of friends growing up who spoke other languages or who came from another country?
- When was your first trip out of the country? What were your experiences?
- What languages do you speak—polite phrases, classroom competent, conversational, or completely fluent?

④ Connect the dots in your **business experience**. You may surprise yourself. You have more international experience, directly or indirectly, than you think!

- What past international experience do you have?
- What indirect international experience do you have? Even if you did not work directly in international business, exposure can provide valuable insight.

Chapter 2

Add Value

In those hazy thoughts between wake and sleep, Alex struggled, feeling trapped. He worried about the push and pull, shove and yank, of company and customers. The company's ambition to enter new markets contrasted with the force of new customers. Without customers, the business would die. Alex often felt ensnared in this dilemma.

Each new US market presented different challenges for TolpaTek. As the company expanded into new industry sectors, the staff found that each sector viewed its business problems in a different way. Tossing and turning, this created many sleepless nights for Alex. TolpaTek offered equivalent products and services across industries, but customers did not view the priorities, solutions, or problems alike.

It was a conundrum. Yes, TolpaTek offered equivalent features and capabilities, but each customer in a different industry viewed TolpaTek's value and impact to his or her company uniquely. How could customers be so vastly different—in the same country, with the same currency, the same language, and similar problems?

It took some time, but Alex and his team cracked the code. TolpaTek changed its discovery process to better reveal the <u>gap</u> customers experienced *between their current operations and improved performance with TolpaTek. Since customers viewed the impact and outcome differently, TolpaTek's key to success was the ability to better align with* ***why*** *customers buy. Finally, a good night's sleep; this insight will be key to unlocking international markets.*

Some members of TolpaTek's executive team think that selling their products and services in the United States was straightforward. Alex doesn't like the word "easy" because it minimizes the important thought, strategy, and sleepless nights that went into TolpaTek's US business. The important lessons learned in entering new US markets would help reduce barriers and flatten speed bumps on their journey into new countries.

Add Value for Customers in the *New* Market

Deliver value to customers, and they will reward you with their orders. Your organization will gladly invest in opportunities that bring value to the company. If you deliver exceptional value, it is likely that exceptional success will come your way.

No customers = no business; it is just that straightforward. **If you don't have customers, you don't have a business.** Yes, you can start a business and build all the infrastructure, but without customers, a business is only a skeleton without a nervous system, heart, or blood flowing in its veins.

If you **offer value** to customers,
they will **buy** your products and/or services,
thereby building your business.

If you **bring value** to customers,
they will repay you with their **endorsement**,
case study, or willingness to share business outcome and results.

If you **create value** for customers,
they will reward you with their **loyalty**,
continuing to do business with you over time.

If you **deliver value** to customers,
they will give you **referrals**,
opening doors to new customers and new opportunities.

An **accelerator** for your business is to provide valued benefits to your customers. Value is the impact that products and services have for them or their business. Impact is the measureable value you create in your customers' businesses or in their lives. Results are what's most important to your customers. It's what your customers get in return for buying and using your products or services. The greater the results and impact, the greater value and higher priority your products and services will have in-country.

Find the Value Gap

Customer value is a business basic. Too often we wave off the notion of value—"of course we add value"—then go on discussing technology, innovations, and process. When moving into a new market, especially a new international market, the notion of value is *paramount.* The value your company delivers in one market is not a direct translation into a new market, especially when moving into international markets or new industry sectors.

Value is perception: how you communicate about your products and services informs your customer base of the value of your product. Value is all of the expectations you set with images, words, and examples. It's both *how* you talk and *what* you say. What you publish, text, share on Facebook, and tweet lets customers in your new market understand what you are offering.

Value encompasses all of the features and capabilities of your products and services. It's both what you do and how you do it. It's the built-in technology—the science and expertise provided by all the smart people behind the scenes—and the functionality of the proven processes and methodologies your company has tested out.

Value is the benefit or benefit*s* that your products and services deliver. It's the customers' perception of advantage to them. How does your stuff make their business or their lives better? Value is what is important to them (not to you).

The best way to define the **value** for customers in the new market is to connect with them.

* How do customers in-country talk about their needs and what is important to them?
* What features and capabilities will customers in the local market use? What country-specific considerations are important?
* Which benefits are *measureable, significant,* and *important* to customers in-country?
* What are local customers doing or using today, and why?

In the 1970s, Ernesto Sirolli worked with an Italian NGO (nongovernmental organization) in Zambia.[6] Everyone had great intentions and truly wanted to help, yet every project ended in failure. In their travels throughout Zambia, the NGO personnel came to the lush Zambezi River area. They were amazed that, in such a rich fertile valley, the locals had no agriculture.

The NGO saw a fantastic opportunity to introduce agriculture to the people. The staff would teach the Zambian people how to grow Italian tomatoes and zucchini. But, their efforts were met with indifference and disinterest. So, with the best of intentions, the NGO decided to motivate the local Zambians by paying them to attend classes and work in the fields. Some locals showed up, although not many, but the NGO knew the results would later convince the many skeptics.

Instead of asking, "*Why aren't the Zambians growing anything in this rich soil?*" these well-intentioned NGO staff members said to each other, "Thank God we are here—just in the nick of time to save the Zambian people from starvation."

Everything grew beautifully. Beautiful hardy green plants. Rich luscious tomatoes and zucchini. The NGO staff joyously told the Zambians, "Look how easy agriculture is!"

The NGO was proudly watching over the fields. The zucchini were prosperous and large. The tomatoes were plump, red, and ripe. The flavor of the few first vegetables to ripen was divine! Then, the ground seemed to shake. Dozens and dozens of hippos came out of the Zambezi River and decimated every ripe tomato and zucchini in sight. They stomped on plants so that nothing but a green mud soup remained.

The NGO workers shrieked to the Zambians, "My God, the hippos!"

The Zambians calmly replied, "Yes, that is why we have no agriculture here."

"Why didn't you tell us?" asked the NGO workers in shock and dismay.

The Zambians, composed and pragmatic, replied, "You never asked."

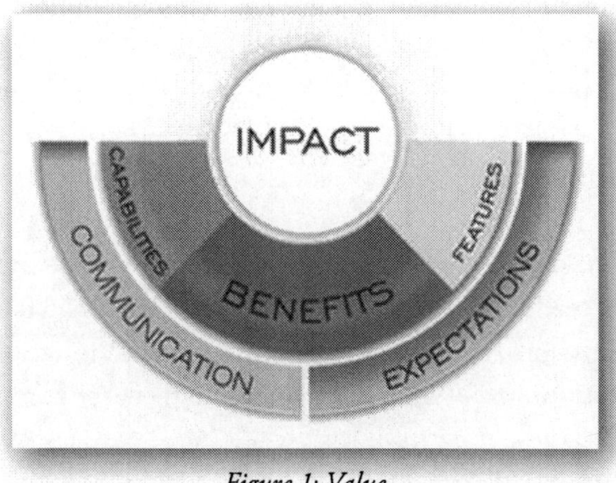

Figure 1: Value

If your offering is agriculture in a country with rich, fertile valleys, does it meet the needs and challenges of the country?

If your product offering is a bicycle, what are the *specific* transportation needs of prospective customers? Countries with good paved roads would have different requirements from countries without them. Get specific. Bicyclists in a relatively flat country like the Netherlands don't need a lot of gears, whereas those in a mountainous country like Switzerland would require a good gear package. People in Singapore might have more disposable income to afford an expensive advanced bicycle, while those in Vietnam might not. Get even more specific and dial in for clarity. An advanced country with sophisticated engineering talent, like Germany, would be able to service a high-tech bicycle, but an emerging country, like Senegal, might not have the available expertise.

If your product offering is a household appliance, what are needs and considerations of the country you are targeting? American homes are large with readily available electricity and ample space. In Japan, living space is at a premium; homes are significantly smaller and might not be able to accommodate a new appliance. Homes in the emerging market countries of Africa may need your household appliance, but may not have reliable access to power or water.

A Story over Coffee with Kevin McCoy

Kevin McCoy's mobile app company was six years old and building a strong following in the United States, so Kevin thought that timing was right to take the business international. Kevin took time to do his homework. He inherently understood important de-risk concepts of ***Built for Global****: starting with English-speaking countries and launching one country at a time. He would test-market in New Zealand, before launching in the United Kingdom, followed by Ireland.*

User experience was a good fit in each of the countries. But, there was no big celebration; it was a lot of work. There were many subtle and not-so-subtle value differences between US and international business. User interaction for this mobile wellness app required distinct country modifications. Users had different preferences for pop-ups and notifications. Each country spoke English, but many things were different: holidays, food preferences, idiomatic expressions, and even units of measure for weight: kilos, stones, or pounds (lbs.).

Obesity is an epidemic in the United States, but that's not the case in other countries. In the United States, health and wellness is all about tracking calories and changing behavior. Other countries think of health and wellness more as lifestyle. Also, some cultures such as Germany and Japan are detailed trackers, whereas others such as the United Kingdom and Ireland are more carefree.

It's not enough to just declare your products and services are available in another country or in the app store. Kevin found that, even with limited resources, his apps needed to be promoted. This was the number-one health-and-wellness app in the United States, but in the United Kingdom, his company was still too small to get the attention of Apple and Google. Kevin leveraged his US relationships to make introductions and get his company's app featured in the new markets.

Kevin is proud of what the company has accomplished in each market, being nimble to adjust to subtle and not-so-subtle user-experience needs. The company continues its agile approach to new markets, moving beyond B2C individual needs and into the unique world of B2B corporate wellness needs.

Be honest in your product assessment. Some products will not meet the needs of certain world markets. We agree with Mona Pearl in *Grow Globally* that you cannot assume a popular product that is performing well in the United States will be successful or suitable in another world market.[7] Kevin McCoy's business is successful and growing outside the United States, but it may not be quite as big as he initially forecast and might have a slightly different market appeal.

Write down your value proposition for the *new* market. A good starting point is a successful value proposition in an existing market, but expect the new market to be different. Sometimes the differences are dramatic, and other times they are more subtle. Your value proposition must speak to the customers in the *new* market—in *their* context...in *their* words.

There are lots of great methodologies for developing a value proposition. We like SRI International's straightforward formula for building a value proposition.[8] SRI International has a long and distinguished history of research and development. Innovations ranging from the computer mouse to Apple's Siri to Intuitive Surgical's robotic surgery grew out of the SRI labs.

SRI International's formula for a value proposition answers four questions:

* What is the customer *need*?
* What is your *approach* to addressing this need?
* What are the *benefits per costs* of your approach?
* How do those benefits per costs compare to those of the *competition*?

These four questions are referred to as "N-A-B-C" for ***n***eed, ***a***pproach, ***b***enefits per costs, and ***c***ompetition. These four elements need to be present in order to create a compelling value proposition.

Here's an example of a B2C (business-to-consumer) value proposition taken from the Arm & Hammer website (www.armandhammer.com) for one of its products, a refrigerator air filter.

> "Arm & Hammer FRIDGE FRESH™ takes Baking Soda out of the back of the fridge and out of the box [*competition*]. It sticks to the inside of your refrigerator [*approach*] and exposes two times more odor-eliminating [*need*] Baking Soda than a regular one pound box [*benefit-per-cost*]."

There are lots of great value proposition examples for B2B (business-to-business) companies too. They will tend to be more industry and application specific due to the complexity of their business.

> *Like many companies, TolpaTek attends relevant industry conferences. TolpaTek is a B2B offering and might use an N-A-B-C value proposition as an introduction. For example, the employees introduce TolpaTek's products to prospective customers with a value proposition like this:*
>
> *"Businesses like yours **need** to have flexible and responsive systems. Our **approach** is a unified service providing adaptable, advanced capabilities. The **benefits** are rapid implementation, integration with your existing services, and self-managed operations; unlike **competitive** offerings, which cost more and require expensive service options. If you have a few minutes now, we could discuss your specific business needs."*

Okay, that TolpaTek example lacks sufficient detail and sounds a bit stiff, but you get the idea of how a value proposition in any business can cover the four key N-A-B-C questions.

A value proposition starts with need. If the customer does not need what you have to offer, you don't have a value proposition.

Figure 2: Need is a gap

Need is a gap that your offer fills. Need is a deficiency, something that is missing, lacking, or not functioning properly in the customer's current situation. The value gap is the difference between the customer's current state and preferred state, in the customer's perception. The greater the perceived difference, the wider the gap. **The wider the gap, the greater the need**, and the higher priority it becomes for the customer to close the gap.

What creates the value gap is unique to each product and service; it could be objective or subjective. The most powerful gaps are created by painful problems.

* Are there consequences that threaten personal or business well-being if the problem doesn't get solved?
* Is addressing this problem required by regulation, certification, or compliance?
* Will someone get fired if the problem isn't solved?

The gap could be very concrete and measureable, which can be communicated in numbers, comparisons, or demonstrations. For example, a company offering Internet service with higher download speeds or wider bandwidth than competitors will be sure to tout the numbers and compare the performance.

The gap could be subjective and individual, based on unproven concepts or personal opinion. Subjective needs are very important and powerful to specific individuals. There are huge industries built on closing the subjective gaps, such as the cosmetics industry in the United States, which is valued at $56 billion plus. Subjective and personal needs often fall within three areas:

* image—personal or company brand;
* Well-being—health, sustainability, or environmental concerns; and
* Status—association, belonging, leadership, or position.

Many products offer a combination of both tangible, demonstrable attributes along with intangible, subjective ones—like a motorcycle manufacturer focusing on both performance and style.

The advantage of closing the gap is also unique to each product or service. Customers may be looking for *payback* or positive returns on investment. For example, faster computer response time or compliments from friends on a more youthful look. Alternatively, the value may be in *avoiding risk* or negative consequences—not being able to run desired computer programs or accelerated aging. Some products, like a motorcycle, may offer a combination of advantages, such as improved fuel efficiency (payback) and safety (risk avoidance).

Your customers in the new market must be made aware of the gap and understand that your product offer will fill it. Entering a new market, you will have to educate potential customers. But…you must educate yourself first.

* There is a gap between your customers' current situation and a preferred state.
* The preferred state offers value/benefits to which they do not currently have access.
* Your product or service fills the gap.
* Acquiring your product or service delivers the desired value, closing the gap. Thus, you deliver value for the customer in the new market.

Your value proposition must speak both the jargon and the local mind-set in-country. You need to do more than just translate it from English to Japanese (or whatever language). Your value proposition should communicate using the terminology of the customers' current business environment—using words that they use. Speak in *their* terms, not your own (and do not use the language of other markets). In this way you will capture their attention and their interest—and, therefore capture their business.

Sometimes your value proposition may merely elicit a response like "What do you mean?" Still, you have started a conversation. This can lead to customer recognition that you bring value, filling a gap that you recognized, but they did not.

The Law of the Four Whys

How do you figure out customer value in the new country? It's customer science, not rocket science. Talk with customers, partners, and your mountain guide in-country. Remember, value is from the customer's point of view. Assess the suitability of your product offering from the customer's perspective.

You cannot understand value in a vacuum. You can't understand value in Chile, China, or Croatia sitting in your comfortable American office in Austin, Boston, or Madison.

Talk with prospective customers in-country. Your goal is to understand important customer needs. Learn the underlying reason "why" your product or service is important to them. Robert and Janet call it the Law of the Four Whys. The Four Whys build importance, starting from your core product features and their capabilities, resulting in customer value and outcome. Outcome and impact are what's most important to your customer.

If you ask your customers the Four Whys, the conversation might sound like this:

Why #1: "Mr. Customer, *why* would you buy from us?"
Answer #1 ➔ "Your offering has the features we were looking for."

* This is helpful; you are learning the **features** that matter to your customer.

Why #2: "Ms. Customer, *why* are those features significant to you?"

Answer #2 ➔ "The features provide the capability for us to do *blah-blah-blah*."

* This is good; you are learning what the features will do for your customers or their business. The focus here is on **functionality** that positively affects workflow or process.

Why #3: "Mr. Customer, *why* is the capability to do *blah-blah-blah* valuable to you?"

Answer #3 ➔ "The capabilities allow our business to do *this and that*."

* This is really getting good. When the customer starts talking about how it *affects her/his business*, you are hearing the **value** the customer is receiving. You will hear comments related to innovation, differentiation, improvement, ROI (return on investment), customer acquisition, customer retention, and the like. If these can be quantified, it is all the more valuable to your understanding. Turn these into a customer case study, and it becomes a valuable proof point for new prospective customers.

Why #4: "Ms. Customer, *why* is doing *this and that* important to your business?"

Answer #4 ➔ "*This and that* contributes to our company growth, profitability, market position, or other business driver in the following ways..."

* Now, you have gotten to the essence of what's really important. The customer is talking about impact and business **outcome**. If the customer is a bank, this is how the bank can grow its business, provide shareholder value, differentiate itself to customers, improve competitive ranking, and more. Can you help the bank become a better bank (or whatever business become better)? The outcome and impact is measured over time.

Warning—if you were really having this conversation in just this way, you might annoy your customer just like a toddler does with a parent when the child asks "why" four times in succession.

Start by describing the Four Whys for your product and service in the United States. Customer case studies usually contain the essential components for the Four Whys.

The Four Whys of the United States will give you clues to uncovering the whys in the new country you are about to enter. But, you still need to ask customers in-country the Four Whys, or you will likely miss the mark.

Figure 3: The Four Whys

Features and attributes are typically the core of ***your*** product offering. But for customers, the core is the impact and outcome for ***their*** businesses. Features and attributes turn into capabilities and functions as customers use them. Capabilities and function produce value and benefits that yield demonstrable impact and positive business outcomes.

Customers most value the impact and outcome; that's why we illustrate them at the center (think of getting to the tasty center of a Tootsie Pop). Unfortunately, many companies focus more on features and attributes (the hard exterior of the Tootsie Pop) than they do on impact and outcome (the real treat in the center). This is obvious in many company websites and marketing collateral.

Answering the Four Whys is equally important as an exercise for understanding and attracting partners in your customer chain as well. Upon entering a new country, you want to attract business partners early in the process because they have access to customers, buyers, and users in-country. Partners may also be necessary to add value or to complete your solution.

TolpaTek works with partners that are system integrators who will sell, implement, and maintain systems. In attracting new business partners, Alex's partner management team will have a "Four Whys" discussion with the leadership team of a prospective system integrator. That discussion might sound something like this:

Why #1: "Mr. Partner, ***why*** *is teaming up with TolpaTek important to you?"*
→ *"Your systems add new capabilities to our portfolio of products and services."*

Why #2: "Mr. Partner, ***why*** *are those new capabilities important?"*
→ *"TolpaTek's capabilities allow us to offer high-end functionality to customers that we weren't able to address previously."*

Why #3: "Mr. Partner, ***why*** *is TolpaTek's high-end functionality valuable to your business?"*
→ *"The high-end functionality leverages our expertise and attracts new customers."*

Why #4: "Mr. Partner, ***why*** *is the leverage of your expertise and attracting new customers important?"*
→ *"We strive to be recognized as the local experts, providing new innovative offerings, to better serve our customers."*

Okay, Alex and his team probably shouldn't ask the Four Whys so directly, but you can see that doing so uncovers what is really motivating Mr. Partner to do business with TolpaTek. It is *not* about the features and capabilities. Mr. Partner's "why" is because of the impact and outcome—helping him build company image and grow the business.

The more unique and differentiated your product or service is within the country, the easier it will be to communicate the Four Whys. Aligning your business with the business of your customers and partners is essential for success.

Stand Out in the Crowd

We live in a crowded and busy world, overflowing with advertising messages—online, in print, and on the street. Shelves are crowded with alternatives, whether you sell steel shipping containers or snacks. Your ability to distinguish yourself in the crowd is important to both you and your customers.

Your success in the US market today is based on your ability to successfully navigate the fast-paced, highly competitive American marketplace. Today's buyer is savvy and demanding. Customers research competitive offerings and expect you to be able to clearly state why your offering is better than another one. Not just better, but truly different and able to deliver compelling results.

Know your competition. Know your competition in the new market. Your marketing department can be a huge help here. Marketing is a core competency of US businesses. Leverage the marketing professionals' extensive knowledge and resources; they have in-depth competitive reports, industry studies, and detailed matrices far beyond what most of the company sees. No, they are not holding back information, just prioritizing for the main competitors encountered in a particular market. Let them know what country you are targeting and which competitors are present. They will surely be able to help with comparative data.

Expect to encounter a very different competitive landscape from what you experience in the United States. The target country may have some unique alternatives, ranging from an in-country solution to competitors from other countries that you haven't confronted before.

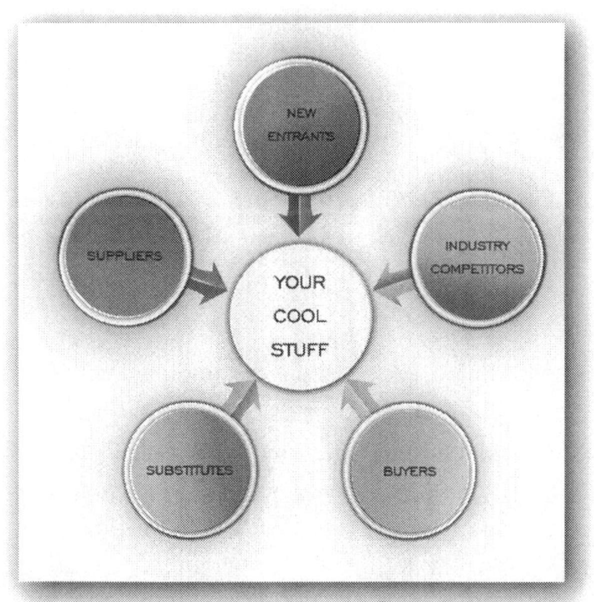

Figure 4: Porter's Five Forces of Competition

If you want to take a deep dive into competitive analysis, pick up a copy of Michael Porter's *Competitive Advantage.*[9] He carefully defines five forces of competition that every industry encounters in some manner: the threat of substitutes, the bargaining power of buyers, the bargaining power of suppliers, rivalry among existing competitors, and the entry of new competitors. The combined strength of these five competitive forces will determine the opportunity of a company to be successful in a given market.

Customers always have options, even if they aren't exactly the same as what you are offering. What are they? Customers want a choice, and they always have alternatives. If the market is growing rapidly, you probably don't need to worry about the options. If the market is big enough, you also may not need to worry much about the alternatives.

Your morning cup of coffee or tea is a great example of why options and alternatives should not worry you in a large or growing market. If you prefer a sweet cup of coffee or tea, use white sugar. If you like it natural, brown sugar, raw sugar, or honey would be preferred. Or, if you are looking for sweetener without calories, you might choose something like Splenda, Sweet 'N Low, or Equal. Or, if you desire natural sweetness without calories, you will look at sweeteners derived from stevia. One cup of coffee or tea, and you can easily see ten or more options and alternatives that comfortably co-reside in their competitive market.

In the competitive world of product options, relative feature performance is important (such as calories, naturalness, and taste). There might also be some switching costs (price, shelf life, or storage considerations). Sometimes the reasons are purely subjective and defy reason (taste, appearance, or consistency).

If the market is static or declining, your new product offering needs to disrupt, revolutionize, or "kick up some dust" to get noticed. **If you can't provide compelling advantage in a static market, don't waste your time or money.**

The vacuum cleaner business in the 1990s is a good example of a dead and dying market. Totally boring. Yawn. James Dyson tinkered with 5,127 vacuum cleaner prototypes in a workshop behind his house before he declared that one worked perfectly. Who knows why he did that, but in 1993 he founded Dyson Ltd. and twenty years later declared £6 billion ($10.2 billion USD) in revenue. He entered a stagnant market in 1993 filled with well-respected brand-name manufacturers like Bissell, Hoover, Electrolux, and others whose world market had never even considered the B-word (billion). Dyson continues to innovate in all areas of its product from suction to filtration to mobility to design. If the company doesn't continue to innovate, it too will stagnate and lose market share.

The customers of today are bossy, demanding, and better informed than ever before. They demand information. They issue RFIs (requests for information), RFPs (requests for proposal), tenders, and RFQs (requests for quotation). They will spend time researching options and alternatives. They want to compare how things will function if they stop doing what they are doing today and start doing what you propose.

The number one competitive **barrier**, above all others, is buyer inertia. Even though your offering is really amazing (we know that what you offer is amazing because that's what you tell us), buyers just may not see it that way. It's just not compelling enough to switch from what they are doing today. Buyers may see and understand what your offering is, but choose not to buy.

Remember when you last switched from one major brand of smartphone to another? You couldn't do things as fast, even the simple stuff. You couldn't find your favorite app, your calendar or contacts weren't brought over, and things functioned differently. You had to unlearn and then relearn. It was a pain! You will think about this before you switch smartphone brands again. Your customers do the same thing. Are you offering something big, really BIG, compelling, and awesome that will make all that pain worthwhile? Ms. Decision-Maker does not want to take a lot of grief for her decision or lose her job.

You are competing for money in buyers' wallets. They have other priorities to spend their money on. In early, emerging countries, spending priorities are likely to focus on fundamentals that address basic survival needs such as water, food, shelter, safety, electricity, or health. In later-stage, advanced countries, spending priorities are wildly different, focused on self-expression, environmental protection, creativity, entertainment, access to information, and/or participation in decision-making. It's a matter of priorities. You are competing with *their* priorities, *their* sense of urgency, and *their* concerns—not yours.

When you enter a new country, don't expect your move to go unnoticed. If this is the first new country your company is entering, you may be able to operate under the radar for a while, but success will bring market visibility to your efforts. Or you may encounter in-country competitors that mount a campaign against you. Keep your head up and eyes open; you never know what you will encounter.

Build a picture of the current competitive landscape:

* What competitors are in this country today?
* What market share is held by each?
* What are the industry trends, in-country and globally?
* How do competitors differentiate or segment themselves in-country?

Uncovering the competitive dynamics in-country is not always easy. An in-country representative, or mountain guide, is an invaluable tool to help you understand how competitors position themselves. We will introduce you to the concept of adding a mountain guide to your team in chapter 4, "Find a Mountain Guide." Competitive rivalry may be based on dynamics similar to what you deal with in the US market, such as discounting, feature wars, and the like. Or you may find competitive rivalry in other countries to operate dramatically differently.

Expect new competitive dynamics that you are unfamiliar with. Competitors may align with social stratification, long-term relationships, or even under-the-table deals. Rival competitors may avoid clashing with one another by aligning with one social strata, caste, or ethnic group; depending on the product, this dynamic may be operating in India, Southeast Asia, South America, and other regions.

Malaysia, for example, has a rich ethnic diversity split between Muslim Malay, Chinese, and Indian. For B2C consumer goods, this means picking your sweet spot for customer focus. For B2B or B2G (business-to-government) goods, it means understanding the business structure. In general, Muslim Malay lead government, universities, halal businesses, and others. Chinese lead retail, import/export, or other commercial business, and Indians provide much of the backbone of labor. Competitors may choose to align with one group and fundamentally ignore another; it is a very different competitive dynamic than we find in the United States.

Home-grown or in-country competitive solutions may present a particularly tough **barrier**, even if they are inferior to your offering. In some cases, local competition may seem to defy logic, and you'll think, "Once we educate the market, they will be eating out of our hand." That may be true, but carefully examine these local drivers. National pride, political connection, cultural context, or government support of competitive alternatives may provide barriers or speed bumps for your business.

Many companies from emerging markets are poised to become important twenty-first century multinationals. Here are examples of some companies on the rise:

* Brazil: Embraer, Sadia & Perdiago, Natura
* Mexico: America Movil, Grupo Modelo
* India: Ranbaxy, Infosys, Tata Tea, WIPRO
* China: Galanz, Haier, Chunlan Group, Lenovo, Pearl River Piano
* Turkey: Koç Holding, Vestel

Arm & Hammer may have difficulty introducing its refrigerator deodorizer into an Asian country where buyers use a local herb with deeply rooted cultural ties even if that herb is more expensive and significantly less effective. TolpaTek may find countries, like France or Singapore, with strong regulatory bodies that are difficult to penetrate due to an intricate web of personal and political connections, as well as strong national pride.

You are the new competitor as you enter a new country. Porter[10] artfully points out that there are a lot of barriers to taking on a new market: brand identity, switching costs, capital requirements, government policy, competitive retaliation, and more. If it was easy, everyone could do it. This is why your boss wants you to work on this problem. *Built for Global* is here to help!

A major **accelerator** is to make your offering *big*, compelling, and awesome by "owning" a process. When you own a process or critical element in a process, it is easier for you to pitch, easier for in-country partners to position, and easier for your customers to understand. It puts you in control. Be clear about what you offer and how it provides a unique methodology for the in-country market.

Initially TolpaTek focused its products and services on IT managers, who are vital to system implementation. TolpaTek had studied the US market, and this strategy aligned with the competitive landscape focused on IT infrastructure and systems management. But, in the early years, TolpaTek was just not getting noticed. The company's products and services offered unique capabilities but just weren't getting much traction among all the "noise" in the market.

A shift in US strategy made all the difference. TolpaTek altered its approach to focus on users, because users played a strategic role in business process decisions. This shift clarified business outcome, embedded TolpaTek's capabilities in the workflow, and allowed it to "own" the process.

* *TolpaTek found its greatest success in the United States with businesses that have complex client relationships—a distinctive customer profile.*

* *The company developed workflow and ROI calculations—tools to help users connect with the value proposition in a meaningful way.*
* *TolpaTek's focus on the business process was a clear differentiator—its competitive advantage.*

Since the focus on user impact and business process provided TolpaTek with compelling advantage in the United States and Canada, the company assumed that this same strategy would serve it well as it entered other advanced countries like Singapore and South Korea. That seemed to make sense as TolpaTek assessed these new markets from the comfort of its US offices, but this was ***wrong****! TolpaTek just couldn't seem to get traction in Singapore or Korea.*

What TolpaTek failed to do was to ask in-country customers the Four Whys. After some disappointing results in these new markets, TolpaTek realized that there was a value shift in the competitive landscape. Competitive comparison was based on different criteria and a different set of competitive offerings. Yes, users were vital to system implementation, but IT managers played a more strategic role in key business process decisions. The products and services were the same, but the value proposition flipped from users back to IT managers.

Dealing with competition is a business basic. When entering a new market, **expect unfamiliar competitive dynamics**. Competitive landscape should be a serious consideration on the diagnostic checklist for country entry. **Markets behave differently**, even when other characteristics seem to be similar. Expect to identify competitors and decision-makers that you may not have encountered before.

Add Value to Your Company

Balancing the excitement of entering new markets with strategic planning can be a challenge. Start with a series of small steps to study, and select the right countries. Carefully consider the important small steps for market entry, delivery, and learning before entering the next new country.

The allure of an international opportunity presenting itself to your company is undeniable. In fact, that is how many companies make their first move into a new country. It could start with a random contact at a trade show or a request for information. Capitalize on opportunities while at the same time maintaining a mindful selection process.

In selecting a new international market to enter, businesses are faced with two somewhat competing goals: feasibility and value. You want a high likelihood of business success along with a sizeable contribution to company revenues or profit. Instead, we would like you to look at feasibility from a different perspective.

Think of feasibility as the degree of difficulty of entering a new market. Consider starting in markets that are easier to penetrate so that your company can gain valuable international experience before tackling larger or more challenging markets.

Think of value as reputation, references, and endorsements. In international markets, reputation is *everything*; company revenue and profit are outcomes. Success is important, but initial revenue numbers are not as important as the beneficial impact your offering has for customers; growth follows real customer value.

The Small-Step Approach

View your entry into a new country as a series of small steps, not a big, all-or-nothing commitment.

* **The market-entry steps:** Are prospective customers aware of your offering? Are customers responding with interest to your offer? Is interest turning into proposals? Are proposals turning into purchases?

What are you learning from each market-entry step? What's different about attracting customers in this new country?

* **The market-delivery steps:** How are products and services delivered and installed? How do customers learn how to use them? What value do customers receive from your products and services? Will customers work with you to document and quantify the value? Will they introduce you to other prospective customers? Will customers endorse your product? What are you learning from each delivery step? What are the unique attributes of the value gap in this country?

* **The learning steps:** Define the next steps for market expansion and market penetration. Celebrate and learn from each small win. Evaluate and learn from your mistakes. If you don't identify what you will do differently next time, you are doomed to repeat the same mistakes. Look beyond customer acquisition to identify what helps you retain customers and build brand loyalty in-country.

The small-step approach should be applied to your international business plan. Take it one country at a time. Set conservative targets for market entry, market delivery, and market expansion. Align investment to expectations, knowing that you will need to invest ahead of demonstrable results. Be optimistic. Be patient. Be realistic.

The small-step approach should be applied to your internationalization plan. Don't plan to expand your business into Asia. Asia includes fifty countries, and spans great distances, from the Mediterranean Sea to the Pacific Ocean, and from the Indian Ocean to the Arctic. Asia spans national borders with great cultural diversity, from Turkey to Russia, China, Japan, and more. Even the further defined subset of Southeast Asia includes twelve or more countries, each with its own unique language, culture, and monetary system: Singapore, Thailand, Vietnam, and others. Pick just one country to begin. Better yet, pick one region/province/state within a country.

One country. Small steps. Incremental milestones and targets for market entry, market delivery, and, much later, market expansion and market penetration.

Start from a Position of Strength

In business, as in life, start from a position of strength. Business expansion is far easier and less risky if you can leverage a current strength into a new area.

A Story over Coffee with Andrew Cadwell

Like a child throwing a tantrum on the floor at the supermarket, sometimes international expansion does not happen with calm sophistication.

Andrew Cadwell's division was entirely focused on the United States. Business was robust and growing. The company distinguished itself in developing deep relationships with large US companies. These large companies also had international operations and were global players.

Customers wanted (even demanded) Andy to provide the same trusted services to their other locations around the globe. The challenge was dropped on the table: "adapt to international business, or accept slower growth and remain down-market."

Andy was the division president of this managed IT solutions and networks services company; Andy decided that his division would adapt, leveraging customer relationships to enter international markets. Andy says "kicking and screaming" more accurately describes the initial international expansion, but the result was leverage and growth.

Other divisions and the entire company later followed suit. Starting from a position of strength, Andy found his current customers to be powerful door openers—lever point one. This also evolved into a formidable barrier to entry for competitors.

The company had no real international experience and decided on a simple, straightforward approach. It would send its US IT and network experts as needed to architect and implement systems, partnering with local suppliers to purchase required hardware and software. In this way they leveraged the strength of their US depth of expertise—lever point two. It seemed simple enough.

However, the road was bumpy in these new markets. There were customer speed bumps; some customers wanted Andy to ship fully configured systems from the United States, while others wanted to use in-country suppliers. There were supplier speed bumps, from product lead time to configuration problems. Andy's business operates on a lean margin, so the bumpy road of delays, currency exchange, value-added taxes, fees, shipping, and receiving could add up. If not carefully managed, the company could actually ***lose*** *money on a project.*

It took some time, but Andy's company worked through all the speed bumps. The company's international business became very profitable and, important to their largest clients, proved that the company could address business challenges "at scale."

Andy's company started from a position of strength, leveraging its core expertise and customer relationships to open new markets.

Andy credits six vital measures to his company's continued long-term international success.

1. *Hire a team fully dedicated to international business.*
2. *Build an international cost calculator to understand potential profitability; include taxes, fees, shipping costs, and delays.*
3. *Enter a country with a dedicated resource.*
4. *Enter a country directly or with partners; don't straddle the fence.*

5. *Don't be afraid to ask for help; retain legal counsel in-country.*
6. *Establish an international customer support line, an extension of point number one above. It builds trust with customers and partners because they can reach out and have a conversation with a human being who will help with questions or problems.*

When taking a company international, Andy recognized the importance of adding value (6 above), reducing risk (2 and 5), finding a mountain guide (3 and 4), building trust (4 and 6), and establishing commitment at all levels (1, 4, and 6). Applying what he learned, Andrew Cadwell has continued a high level of success in his international business ventures.

To find a position of strength, examine these four basic questions:

1) What existing products and/or services do you intend to export?
2) Which new market (new country or state/region) will you be entering?
3) Who is the customer for those products and services? In the US market today? In the new country?
4) What products already exist in the same or similar form in-country?

The most predictable business **accelerator** is to take an existing product into a new or adjacent market to capture new customers. Andy's story above used existing products and leveraged existing customers along with in-house expertise to successfully enter new countries. The best approach to entering a new international market is to use current company strengths—known product features, capabilities, and value—thereby taking as much "newness" out of the equation as possible. If you can also leverage current customers, as Andy did, it is an added bonus.

Expect a few **speed bumps** if you are developing new products to launch within current markets. Knowing your customers and understanding the market reduces the number of variables, which will lessen risk, easing you over the bumps in the road.

The biggest **barrier**, highest risk, and most difficult move is for a company to develop entirely new products for new customers in new countries. In a strict cost-benefit analysis, the risks are far too great. There are just too many unknowns. This, by definition, is what a start-up does, even if the "start-up" is taking place within a well-established company. Twenty-five percent of start-ups fail in the first-year, and fifty percent fail within five years. Take the start-up risk out of the equation; new product for new countries should *not* be your approach to entering a new international market. Remove the barrier, and improve your odds for international success by having only one "new thing" in the mix—take an existing product into a new market, or take a new product into an existing market.

Start from your position of strength. You are achieving success in the US market today with your products and services. Do an internal assessment, and search for products and services suitable for foreign markets.[11] Snoop around marketing and sales to find opinions, information, and documents to direct your efforts.

Figure 5: Taking products to market

For some products and services, the definition of the customer is straightforward because the buyer and the user are the same. When Arm & Hammer sells baking soda as a deodorizer for refrigerators, the buyer is the user. The sweet spot of the target market[12] is a homeowner with a refrigerator who refers to him- or herself as successful and shows pride of ownership. The household has enough discretionary income to include nice-to-have items in its shopping list.

When Arm & Hammer considers exporting its refrigerator deodorizer into a country outside the United States, its position of strength is to prioritize countries with the closest alignment to its US sweet spot. Canada, Japan, Singapore, or Australia all have buyers closely aligned with the sweet spot.

For other products and services, the definition of "customer" is far more complex. The buyer may be different from the user. Other partners may be required to complete the offering. If this is the case, it is helpful to diagram the links in the customer chain and identify the sweet-spot characteristics of each link in the chain. Each link of the customer chain must be strong for that product to be successful.

When TolpaTek decided to expand outside of North America, it targeted Asia and, wisely, narrowed down the selection to two countries for initial entry. TolpaTek prioritized Singapore and South Korea because the company could work from a position of strength. The links of the customer value chain closely paralleled those in North America.

TolpaTek could work with local ***partners*** *that were system integrators with the requisite expertise.* ***Buyers*** *and* ***users*** *in these markets closely matched the technology managers and business process owners that TolpaTek worked with in North America, a proven position of strength. There were ample* ***best-fit businesses*** *that managed complex client relationships.*

To ensure your success for new-market entry, document the following four essential items for each product and service:

1. Identify the links in the customer chain.
2. Describe value for each link in the customer chain.
3. Develop a detailed profile (or persona[13]) for the buyer and the use.
4. Articulate the Four Whys.

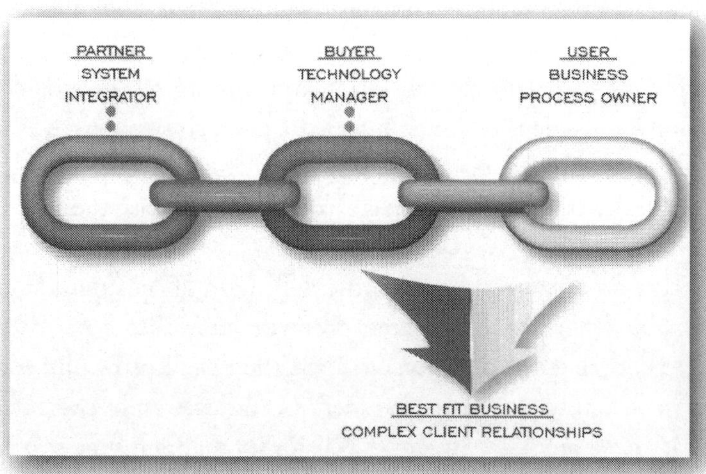

Figure 6: Example of links in the customer chain

Is the Trend Your Friend?

It is far easier to go with the flow than to swim upstream.

Who doesn't love a good trend? Some trends are just fads, here today and gone tomorrow, like fashion trends, pet rocks, reality TV, and celebrities. Hopefully what is going on in your industry isn't a fad.

Other trends extend over time. If your business is linked to important US, global, or country-specific issues, it won't be a passing fad, but a real market trend. Real market trends withstand fads, competitive chaos, and economic roller coasters.

A Story over Tea and Skype with Jik Chu

Spotting or forecasting a trend is tricky. Jik Chu saw firsthand the damaging results of not correctly predicting a trend.

Jik worked for a major US paint and chemical company that was looking to expand and bring its manufacturing and retail model into Asia. Jik was born in Seoul, South Korea. He went to college in the United States and worked for US companies after graduation for fifteen-plus years before returning to South Korea.

The combination of US and Asian experience opened the door for Jik. The commitment to international expansion came from the top. The chairman, international VP, and Jik made four tours through Japan, South Korea, Hong Kong, Taiwan, Philippines, and Indonesia.

The company courted joint venture (JV) partners in Korea and Hong Kong: two prosperous, advancing economies that could support cost-effective manufacturing and potential retail outlets. The Korean partner proposed a JV and factory in South Korea. The Hong Kong partner had already obtained a license from the Indonesian government and proposed building a paint factory in Indonesia.

Market size was a key determining factor. Indonesia's population was over two-hundred million, and South Korea's was just thirty million, 15 percent of Indonesia's. The GDPs of both Indonesia and South Korea were similar at the time. Jik suggested that the company look beyond population size to other emerging trends within each country. The South Korean GDP was expected to grow at more than 10 percent per year, whereas Indonesia expected slower growth of around 3 percent. Additionally, South Koreans had a higher overall education level and a cultural commitment to education. Jik supported the Korean proposal, but the company decided to move forward with the Hong Kong partner and a paint factory in Indonesia.

After just five years the company closed the Indonesian plant, shut down retail stores, and liquidated the JV. Lesson learned for this previously successful paint and chemical company—failure to identify the trends was very costly. Market size alone was not enough. The company did not correctly predict the growth of the two economies. The average household in Indonesia did not have sufficient interest or income to spend in retail paint and decorating stores.

Business glory is having products and services in the vortex of a real market trend with sustained movement over a prolonged period of time. Trends are most clearly seen through the rearview mirror, after they have had enough sustained momentum to measure their impact. The really tough challenge is having the vision to recognize developing trends through the windshield, to anticipate their direction and scope.

Another Story over Tea and Skype with Jik Chu

Missing a trend can have a long-term negative effect on a company. Jik Chu has another story of a "case in reverse" where a company did not recognize the value of a trend.

Wind the clock back to the early era of the mobile revolution. Two fast, up-and-coming start-up companies came to South Korea to court technology companies for investment. One start-up had developed a unique chip set for mobile phones, and the other had created a smartphone operating system (OS).

The start-up with the chip set was seeking $60 million USD in investment. Instead of investing, the Korean company entered into a technology transfer agreement, paying a modest initial license fee with royalties over time. It seemed a wise and low-risk decision at the time. But, the Korean company did not correctly anticipate the development or energy of the mobile revolution. The strength and durability of mobile computing meant that this Korean company eventually paid over $300 million in royalties. Lesson learned for the Korean investor—failure to correctly identify the direction and scope of a trend is very costly.

The start-up with the smartphone OS came to Korea looking for investment, approaching several companies, and each refused. Today, this smartphone OS is the largest revenue generator for a US company. For the Korean companies that refused investment, the licensing fees are staggering, and one company pays billions of dollars USD to use this smartphone OS.

The lesson Jik sees for Korean companies, and others, is this: "When you see a potential technology, grab it. If you don't spot the power of the trend, you will be paying much more later." Jik points out it is not easy to spot trends; it requires good technical judgment and vision. Such vision should not be overshadowed by corporate ego or patriotism, which might encourage the thinking that "we can do this better ourselves."

Today, Jik is a retired executive who acts as a mountain guide for companies wanting to enter South Korea. Jik Chu has many engaging stories to tell, and you will hear more of them in chapter 4, "Find a Mountain Guide."

Early in your decision-making process, explore the trends affecting the country you would like to enter. Pay close attention to

* important issues within the country and
* stage of economic development.

When trends are working in your favor, they will be powerful **accelerators**. They provide pull into a country and generate demand. You can leverage the trends to make contacts, establish in-country partners, and attract customers.

When trends are working against you, they will be **barriers**. In some cases they could be insurmountable barriers. You will have to decide how much risk you are willing to take by bucking the trends.

If the optimist voice in your head says, *"It's a green light; let's go,"* first analyze the level of investment that you are willing to make. Your goal will be to invest the smallest amount of time, money, and people resources to reduce risk and verify that success can be achieved.

On the other hand, be cautious if the idealist voice in your head says, *"It's greenfield; no one else is doing it. We can break new ground, and we will be a trendsetter, not a trend follower."* Yes, there are trendsetters in every industry and every country. We do **not** say, "No, don't do that!" But be cautious. Build a plan, make this country a "controlled experiment," set benchmarks, and establish lever points for stop-loss as well as for increasing investment. Stick to your plan, and monitor it closely. As with the stock market, don't get too emotionally attached to it. We can't deny that there is power in first-mover advantage, but there is also risk. Don't forget the many early American pioneers that were buried en route while heading out to settle the Wild West.

Evaluate the trends. Make good business decisions; good decisions bring you rewards. Bad decisions leave you dusting off your résumé.

Important issues within a country affect people and business and government policy. Read beyond the *Wall Street Journal* and *New York Times*; read the local news. Sign up for Google alerts, and subscribe to an online news source based in the capital city of the country. In the first weeks, *scanning* the articles will illuminate trending topics. In weeks three and beyond, *reading* the articles will give you a deeper understanding of the challenges and opportunities in-country. News stories will also define and quote the people in-country who are central actors. Use your Business 101 detective skills to identify government and business entities involved in addressing the issue. These skills will soon uncover individuals, government agencies, businesses, and foundations trying to solve the problem.

Major issues will be top of mind and top priority on personal, business, and government agendas. Expect to find projects, programs, initiatives, and plans swirling around the important issues. If your product/service offering can have a positive impact on these important issues, this will be an instant launching point and will accelerate your business in-country. This acceleration will be true for any business, B2C, B2B, or B2G.

Stage of Economic Development

Countries and their economy are often segmented into one of the following stages of development:

* advanced (also referred to as industrialized or developed),
* developing, or
* emerging.

The specific stage of economic development and country classification varies depending upon whom you ask. The United Nations, IMF (International Monetary Fund), World Economic Forum, and other organizations have different criteria for classifying development within a country.

Countries can also move from one classification to another through sustained development, like those listed below as "recently graduated" or "rapidly developing." Countries on the move will likely have policies and initiatives in place that support the advancement of their economy. Most authorities would classify the selected countries as follows:

Advanced	Developing	Emerging
Australia, Austria, Belgium, Canada, Czech Republic,* Denmark, Finland, France, Germany, Ireland, Israel,* Italy, Japan, Latvia,* Netherlands, New Zealand, Norway, Portugal, Singapore,* Slovakia,* South Africa, South Korea,* Spain, Sweden, Switzerland, Taiwan,* Turkey, United Kingdom, and United States	Algeria, Argentina, Belize, Bulgaria, Chile,* Colombia, Ecuador, Egypt, Georgia, Indonesia, Iran, Kenya, Malaysia,* Mongolia, Pakistan, Panama, Philippines, Thailand, Turkey, Ukraine, United Arab Emirates,* Venezuela, Vietnam, and Zimbabwe	*Africa Emerging:** Angola, Burkina Faso, Central African Republic, Chad, Equatorial Guinea, Eritrea, Ethiopia, Gambia, Guinea, Liberia, Mali, Mozambique, Niger, Rwanda, Senegal, Sierra Leone, Sudan, Tanzania, Uganda, and Zambia
Recently Graduated:* Czech Republic (2008), Latvia (2014), and Slovakia (2009)	***Rapidly Developing:**** United Arab Emirates, Chile, and Malaysia	***Asia-Pacific Emerging:**** Afghanistan, Bhutan, Bangladesh, Cambodia, Laos, Myanmar, Nepal, and Yemen
Straddling the Fence "BRIC" or "BRICS" Brazil, Russia, India, and China, including South Africa		***Other Emerging*** Solomon Islands and Haiti

* Rapidly evolving in recent years

Figure 7: Stage of Economic Development[14]

Each classification system provides information that may be of interest to your company as you expand international operations.

* The United Nations' Statistics Division contains a wealth of demographic data including the following: economic, societal, environmental, geographic, energy, age, and gender.
* The IMF (International Monetary Fund) contains a great deal of current and historical statistics on financial, trade, GDP, currency, payments, and more.
* The World Economic Forum provides information on infrastructure, transportation, IT, Internet communications, and innovation, among other things.

When taking your company international, one strategy could be to focus on countries that fall into one of the three classifications: advanced, developing, or emerging. This strategy makes sense from the standpoint that there will be similar characteristics of infrastructure, education systems, and monetary resources. There can also be similar expectations for buyer behavior. Needs, trends, and issues typically align with the stage of economic development.

Emerging countries are often struggling to build basic infrastructure or vital substructure for human existence. Basic infrastructure requirements might include waste disposal, electricity production, transportation, education, health care, and other fundamentals. Vital substructure for human existence might include clean water, food production, air quality, housing, and even basics such as clothing.

Developing nations are often grappling with hyper growth of one type or another. High population growth can stress the job market and housing availability. Rapid development can deplete natural resources, strain infrastructure, and create inequity in delivery of basic services. Accelerated economic growth can be a double-edged problem, creating jobs, especially in economic centers, while draining knowledge resources, management talent, and the labor force from surrounding areas. Rapid economic growth can also create an instantly large and affluent middle class, which, in turn, can lead to the negative effects of rapid population growth, overdevelopment, pollution, and increased crime rates.

Economically **advanced countries** have the fundamental needs addressed for the majority of the population, so issues will focus more on human enrichment and environmental protection. They value access to information, tolerance of diversity, and self-expression, leading to a rising demand for participation in decision-making. People who live in advanced countries have more disposable income. They are looking for products and services that differentiate them personally or professionally.

Emerging and developing markets can be very attractive for your business.

* Emerging and developing markets often exhibit high economic growth rates. A growing middle class has a growing demand for electronics, cars, health care services, and countless other products.

These countries can provide a manufacturing base for a wide variety of products. They offer quality labor at low wage for manufacturing and assembly, like Ethiopia, Cambodia, or Malaysia do. Others, including Brazil, Colombia, or Chile, have significant reserves of raw materials or natural resources.

* They are sourcing destinations for a wide variety of services and know-how. Multinational enterprises have established numerous call centers in Eastern Europe, India, Philippines, and elsewhere. Dell and IBM outsource certain tech functions to knowledge workers in India. Intel and Microsoft have programming centers in Bangalore, India. Investments from abroad benefit emerging markets with new jobs and production capacity, transfer of technology, and links to global markets.

Many analysts predict that the highest percentage of the world's growth in the next two decades will come from the emerging and developing markets, while the advanced economies of the world may struggle.

Developing and emerging markets have the opportunity to *roar.* If the economy of a developing country is highly export driven, with strong inflows of capital and investment, it means that money will be available to spend on the right imports. These could be your product/service offerings if you have uncovered a large and untapped value gap for customers in these emerging markets.

Advanced markets present a strong, solid base of opportunity as well. High per capita income and stable economies are attractive. Buyers are demanding, looking for new and innovative offerings, but they do represent a large identifiable market base.

Hard to Classify

Each country has a unique and complex economic system. The truth is that no country can be neatly classified into only one of these categories. Every country will have advanced areas functioning side by side with emerging or underdeveloped areas, even the United States. Urban areas, big cities, and the capital city will be more developed than sparsely populated rural areas. Important issues facing a country are typically a mixture of multiple levels. There can be a very stark contrast comparing the capital, Kuala Lumpur, with rural Malaysia, just as there is when comparing New York City with rural West Virginia. The countries that comprise BRIC/S (Brazil, Russia, India, China, and South Africa) are perfect examples. The major cities are highly developed and advanced; however, travel farther inland, and you will find poor, agrarian, and underdeveloped areas.

You are the expert in your industry, not us. What trends are accelerating your business in the United States? Are the same trends at play globally, regionally, or in specific countries? You don't need to answer all these questions yourself; tap into your corporate intelligence on industry trends. Marketing can unlock the secrets of global and regional market trends. If your business is more tech driven, look to engineering or product management to unlock tech-trend secrets. If you're in a service business, take the professional services executive out for coffee.

The trend is your friend. If global business is trending in your favor, it is only a matter of time before your target country will embrace it. The big challenge is to get the timing right in each country. Are you looking for the advantage of being the first-mover, a fast follower, or early-majority appeal? Trends, megatrends, and even hyped-up trends can be business accelerators.

If your product or service offering helps to solve or address key issues facing the country, it can be an important **accelerator** for you. The implications are *big*. Real trends can be accelerators for your business moving into international markets. This isn't just a feel-good statement; the degree that your offering can achieve demonstrable, measureable, and quantifiable results can propel the business *dramatically*. Your business can move in *response* to these results, improving growth factors, shareholder value, competitive ranking, and other high-impact outcome. Work to make contact with the movers and shakers on important issues affecting your business and get noticed!

Define and Rate Your Strengths

In this self-assessment, carefully consider key aspects of your value proposition. How does your value proposition connect with partners and customers? Are you working from a position of strength?

Take this assessment to marketing and product marketing, and ask them to *independently* evaluate the company strengths for the new market, providing their perspective on customers, competitors, and trends.

Compare your assessment with those from other departments. Some very interesting insights will emerge. The foundation for your market-entry plan will begin to emerge—leverage your agreed strengths and build up areas that are weak.

In the following assessment, establish your unique definition for "partners." In a B2B (business-to-business) approach, partners could be integrators, value-added resellers, manufacturers, or service providers that combine your offering with their own to bring it successfully to market. In a B2C (business-to-consumer) approach, partners could be retailers, distributors, or service providers with direct consumer contact.

① Value Strength for Your Customer

1. Identify the links of the customer chain for each product and service. Be specific in description or by name.

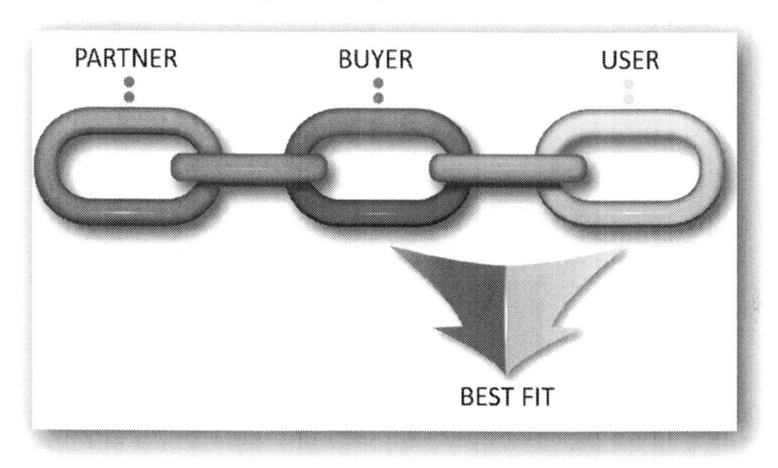

2. Describe your ideal in-country customer:

   * best-fit business profile,
   * ideal characteristics (persona[15]) of the buyer, and
   * ideal characteristics (persona) of the user—if different from the buyer.

   For B2B offerings, be specific about the type of companies representing your ideal buyer, and list names of example companies. Describe ideal business size (number of employees, revenue, other); industry segment; maturity (early stage, in-stride, mature); type of business; and other. Outline the users within the company, by department, job function, title, and other.

   For B2C offerings, be specific about the traits of the individuals representing your ideal buyer and user. Describe relevant characteristics such as gender, age group, income level, education, interests, attitudes, hobbies, urban/suburban/rural, and other.

3. Write out the value proposition for *each link* of the customer chain (question 1 above):

    * What is the value proposition for your in-country partner?
    * What is the value for the buyer?
    * What is the value proposition for the in-country user?

    Use your own format for the value proposition or SRI International's N-A-B-C structure (need-approach-benefits-competition):

    * What is the *partner / buyer / user* **need**?
    * How does your **approach** address this need?
    * What are the **benefits per cost** of your approach for the *partner / buyer / user*?
    * How do these benefits compare to **competitive alternatives** available to the *partner / buyer / user* in-country?

4. For each link in the customer chain, describe the Four Whys in terminology that would be used by partners, buyers and users in-country. Include

    * feature or attribute,
    * capability or function,
    * value and benefit, and
    * impact and outcome.

② Your Starting Position of Strength

1. What country or countries are you considering?
2. What products and/or services do you intend to take international?

    For each product and/or service, answer the following questions. Yes answers put you in a position of strength.
    * Is this an existing product or service?

* If already selling outside the United States, is the new in-country customer profile identical to that of other successful countries?
* If not selling outside the United States, is the in-country customer profile *identical* to that of the United States?

③ Your Competitive Strength

1. Who are the existing competitors?
   a. How do they compete?
   b. How have they divided the market between themselves?

2. What other options, substitutes, or alternatives are being used in-country (other than those listed above)?

3. What are your unique, innovative, and compelling differentiators?

   Rate your relative competitive position in-country: weak, neutral, or strong.
   * How does your offering compare to competitive options and alternatives?
   * Will buyer interest be weak, neutral, or strong?
   * As buyers demonstrate their willingness and ability to buy, what level of interest is expected?
   * What level of importance do you expect from users?

④ The Strength of Your Trend Alignment

1. What are the top five in-country trends affecting people, business, and government?

2. Is your product/service offering aligned with the stage of development needs of the country?

3. List the top five in-country trends.
   Trend 1:
   Trend 2:
   Trend 3:
   Trend 4:
   Trend 5:

4. Are you a laggard, a follower, or a leader? Are you in a weak, average, or strong position?
   * Rate your alignment to the five key in-country trends outlined above.
   * Rate your alignment with the stage of economic development in-country.
   * Rate your alignment with global trends in your industry.

Chapter 3

De-Risk

What's worse? Getting fired or the humiliation? To Mr. Joon-ho Kim, the shame of humiliation was the worst thing that could happen. Suffering that loss of respect among his peers would be unbearable; it would even affect his family. Mr. Kim was apprehensive. Was it a good decision to work with TolpaTek...or not?

TolpaTek found significant interest in its products and services coming from Asia, specifically Singapore and South Korea. One inquiry was developing quite quickly from mild interest to serious investigation. Alex asked Casey, the west coast director, to chase it down.

A Korean tech-system integrator was very interested in the possibility of bringing TolpaTek capabilities into Korea. The company saw great potential and opportunity for their current customers. After multiple discussions and several trips to Korea, the integrator and TolpaTek agreed to work together.

The Korean company wanted the announcement to make a big splash. The company invited three hundred people to a five-star hotel for a Monday morning breakfast, keynote address, demonstration, and press briefings.

This was big! The hotel was the Ritz Carlton in Seoul, Korea, and the three hundred guests represented industry heavy hitters in the region.

Casey's flight arrived on time in Seoul, early Sunday morning, providing him time to acclimate. He planned to shower, fine-tune his keynote address, review the setup, and meet with the partner to discuss any last-minute details.

After arriving at the hotel, Casey was excited, so he decided that the shower could wait and headed straight to the meeting room. It was an elegant, massive room at the Ritz Carlton that would comfortably hold all three hundred industry luminaries. Everything looked great! Mr. Joon-ho Kim, the key contact for TolpaTek's Korean partner, had seen to every detail. The stage was arranged beautifully with the newest technologies for demonstration, presentations, and open forum discussion. All Casey had to do was log in and access the software for tomorrow's demo.

Casey wanted to get comfortable with the process and went online for log-in. A pop-up window appeared. It was in Korean, so Casey asked Mr. Kim to translate. Mr. Kim was stunned. To his disbelief the computer provided for demo access said the systems were not compatible. Yikes! How could this be?

TolpaTek systems were engineered for universal compatibility, or so Casey thought. Korea was leading technology innovation around the globe, and the partner had provided the most advanced hardware and operating system available for this big, high-profile event.

But, TolpaTek systems had not yet been tested for compatibility with this most current release. Yikes! The noise in their heads was shouting

"Now what?" Things were not working. They may have looked composed on the outside, but inside Casey and Mr. Kim were both frantic! The partner had spent tens of thousands of dollars (well over 10 Million Korean won—KRW) on this event, and now they had less than twenty-four hours to figure something out.

Mr. Kim started calling everyone he knew. It was the weekend. It was impossible to get in touch with anyone. Casey started calling tech support for TolpaTek in the United States. It was Sunday, and the office was closed, but there was an on-call engineer to handle emergencies. Casey and Tim discussed the situation. Tim didn't have a solution but called the director of development, who might be working on interoperability. No, unfortunately work had not yet begun in this area, as the technology was not anticipated to hit in the US market until next year.

Casey was distraught but started contemplating Plan B. Perhaps he could do a presentation, talk through the demo, and show a few screenshots. It would certainly not meet the expectations of the audience, but what other choice did he have?

Finally, around three o'clock in the afternoon, Mr. Kim found a colleague in Pusan, about 200 miles (320 kilometers) south of Seoul, who had a compatible setup. Mr. Kim respectfully insisted that Casey remain at the hotel and prepare for the next day. Casey said, "We're in this together" and jumped into the car with Mr. Kim. They headed south; it would be a four-to five-hour drive, each way. It was not all superhighways between Seoul and Pusan, but at least there wasn't any traffic on a Sunday afternoon. They successfully made the trip and picked up the compatible system needed for the TolpaTek demo.

It was five o'clock, (yes, five o'clock in the morning) when Casey and Mr. Kim returned to the Ritz Carlton and had the compatible system in place. No sleep. No shower. Four hours to "show time." Casey got on the phone with engineers in the United States to ensure that everything was functioning properly.

By seven o'clock, everything was working. The dark circles under Casey's eyes were attributed to jet lag. Mr. Joon-ho Kim was quite exhausted but composed. The event turned out to be a huge success, and this partner became one of TolpaTek's top distributors. Casey and Mr. Kim now share a special bond of respect, trust, and friendship, along with their secret, hair-raising story.

Had Casey done a bit more research on Korea or better coordination with Mr. Kim, he might have gotten some sleep the night before that big presentation and demo. The sign of a successful businessperson is one who has learned exponentially from his or her experience. Moral to the story: prepare for the worst. If problems can happen, they will happen, but you will be able to work through them. You can avoid the simple problems. Just do your homework in advance.

Reduce Risk for Your Company

When opportunity knocks, answer the door. "Opportunities are never lost; someone will take the ones you miss."[16]

Most companies begin their international expansion unexpectedly.

It's random. You are at a trade show, and a prospect from outside the United States approaches you to learn more about what you do; it could be a prospective customer or partner. You enter into a great dialog. The person invites you to his or her country to meet with him or her and explore an opportunity to work together.

Opportunity finds you. You receive contact (phone, e-mail, or letter) from a prospective international customer or partner. This person was researching alternatives and found you. You were just going about business as usual and not thinking of taking your company into this country.

You get a request. A current multinational customer or partner enquires about your offering being available to them in other countries where their business is established. Your US salespeople are eager to make a sale and consider the possibility of selling to this company in the United States and letting the customer (or partner) take it from there.

If the opportunity comes from a credible partner, this can be an especially great accelerator for international expansion. This could even be your introduction to an in-country representative, which we will talk more about in the next chapter, "Find a Mountain Guide."

If the opportunity comes from a current or prospective customer, this could be your first sale and launch your sales operations in a new country or region. Examine the possibility that this customer could be your first proof-of-concept customer and reference in-country; there is also more on that in chapter 5, "Build Trust."

Do your homework. Yes, the possibility is exciting, but it's important to vet the opportunity and assess the risk of pursuing it. But, it's a question of balance; don't miss an opportunity with analysis paralysis. **Some countries will be a better fit for your offering than others.** Do your due diligence so that you make an informed decision and are able to successfully support operations in a new country. You don't want to miss out on a good opportunity. Robert says, "Companies that are the best at international business have the most common sense."

Pick Your Spot: One Country at a Time

Companies talk about "going global," "taking the company international," or "expanding into Europe" (or Africa, South America, Asia, or wherever). Sorry to break the news to you, but there are 196 countries in the world, and you can't "go global" like flipping on a light switch or setting a new temperature on the thermostat.

The reason many US companies think that "going global" is a single move is because of the very nature of doing business in America.

- ➔ A flight across the United States from Los Angeles to Boston is 3,500 miles (5,630 kilometers), flying over forty-eight states that use one language and one currency, with some minor regional differences.
- ➔ In contrast, a flight from Portugal to Kazakhstan is a similar distance of 3,800 miles (6,116 kilometers); however, the flight crosses over fifty-two countries that use more than a hundred languages and twelve different currencies.

There is a famous question: "How do you eat an elephant?" The answer: "One bite at a time!" This old African proverb is our approach to going global. Expand globally, **one country at a time**. Expect to start slow and to pick up speed as your company gains needed expertise in regulations, language, currencies, and more.

Going global is more like a rheostat adjusting the brightness of a light progressively or a thermostat slowing changing the temperature. Going global is adding countries gradually, bringing up the international intensity one step at a time.

If you are "expanding into Europe," establish a plan that starts with one country and leverages one or more attributes into another country. Here are some examples of how you might pick your spot and expand into Europe.

1) Compatible trading blocs (the countries share something in common):
    * Choose several countries that share a currency, such as the Euro—select one country; then expand into others, such as Austria, Belgium, Finland, France, Germany, Greece, Ireland, Italy, Latvia, Netherlands, Portugal, Slovakia, or Spain.

  * Choose an intergovernmental cooperation zones, such as Scandinavia—where Denmark, Norway, Finland, Sweden, and others have reduced or eliminated trade barriers and tariffs

2) Language/communication compatibility:
   * Focus on English—start with Ireland; then expand into England and Scotland.
   * Focus on German—start with Germany, later moving into Austria, Switzerland, Luxembourg, Liechtenstein, the eastern cantons of Belgium, and northern Italy.
   * Beyond language compatibility, you might also consider cultural communication and decision-making styles—Japan and South Korea both share a collaborative, group-think culture of decision-making.

3) Compatible geography:
   * Choose countries with shared borders—Switzerland, for example, shares borders (and languages) with France, Germany, Italy, and Liechtenstein; the Swiss people are multilingual, speaking German, French and English.
   * Look for transportation ease—by rail, road, or air with reliable customs, import/export processes.

Pick your spot. Not spots, plural. Going global is done one country at a time; slowly at first and picking up speed over time. Yes, we are repeating ourselves. Has it sunk in yet?

One Country at a Time.

Understand the customers and the market in each country you enter. Austrians are different from Germans, even though they share the same language. Every country is different. France is different from Spain, even though they share a border. Greece will have different problems from those found in England.

Your offering might be viewed as a serious painkiller in Latvia and just a health drink in Ireland.

Political Situation

The political situation of a country is often referred to as "political climate." Why "political climate"? What does politics have to do with the climate conditions? Rather than "climate," a better description might be "political weather" because the variation of political conditions can be volatile and change rapidly, like a fast-moving thunderstorm boiling across the Midwest's Great Plains.

Political relations between the United States and your target country can be a **barrier** to entry. You will have no control over this, so it is the first thing that you should examine. Get a brief history, current status, and projection on future political relationship before you invest time and resources to bring your business into a country. Beware: political alignment can, like the weather, change quickly. If key indicators are that the political weather is deteriorating, it is in your best interest to select another country for your international move.

There are many countries where the pendulum has shifted with the political weather over time. It can affect countries anywhere in the world, big or small. Recent examples are Crimea, Cuba, Venezuela, and Vietnam, just to name a few. The changing political weather in these countries would directly affect your ability to do so. Below are a few examples that illustrate the dramatic shift that political weather can have on your business plans.

> In just the last one hundred years, Crimea has been controlled by at least five different factions. After World War I, Crimea became part of what was later known as the Soviet Union. After World War II, relations with the United States were frozen by the Cold War. In

1954, trade with western nations was relaxed as Crimea was transferred from Russia to Ukraine, though still part of the Soviet Bloc. In 1991, further independence opened up more trade options when Crimea became an autonomous republic within the newly independent Ukraine. In early 2014, Crimea was again on a roller coaster of volatility when Russian troops occupied the country, transferring control back to Russia (again). United States and Russia relations have been tense with economic sanctions and the threat of armed conflict.

Cuba has had strained relations with the United States for many years, in part due to an official government embargo after the communist revolution of 1961. US companies doing business in Cuba lost significant capital in property, manufacturing, and customers when diplomatic ties were severed and economic sanctions enacted. The United States restored diplomatic relations with Cuba in 2015. Although the pendulum is swinging toward a more favorable relationship, business opportunities must still be approached cautiously, as the Cuban embargo remains in place.

Venezuela is on a very bumpy road in its diplomatic relations with the United States. The relationship was strong in the early 1970s, and Venezuela was a popular vacation destination for many Americans. The Venezuelan government had solid connections to the United States for trade, investment, and control of the illegal drug trade. By the late 1990s, however, tensions increased and Venezuela broke off diplomatic relations with the US government. In 2007, the Venezuela government seized oil interests worth billions of dollars; Exxon Mobil and ConocoPhillips left the country and sued for compensation. Currently, economic sanctions remain in place.

Vietnam's relations with the United States are still largely defined by the Vietnam War, which many Vietnamese call the "American War." After twenty painful years of restricted economic and political ties, the relationship between the United States and Vietnam

> was normalized in 1995. Since the reopening of the US Embassy in Hanoi and the US Consulate in Ho Chi Minh City (formerly Saigon), our two countries have continued to broaden political and economic exchange. Although there remain some vivid reminders of the "American War" for the Vietnamese people and of the Vietnam War for US veterans and others, today Vietnam and the United States share a very positive relationship.

The type of government is the framework for how the society operates. This affects how business decisions get made. The level of regulatory controls, private ownership, and other critical factors affect your business. The length of time a government has been in place affects the decision-making process, protocols, and stability. Stability is primarily a subjective measure of the internal acceptance of government practices and principles by dominant factions within the country and other countries doing business with it.

If the political situation looks amenable, it's important to understand several things about the government within the country you are targeting:

* What is the type of government?
* How long has it been in place?
* How stable is it?

Consider how a relationship with the government will affect your business. For instance, a government can support your efforts to import products or open for business within its country. Look to build relationships with ministries or departments of government that regulate your industry. If you will be creating jobs or building expertise within the country, build relationships with the ministry or department of economic development.

However, a positive relationship is not always the case. There can be many hidden currents and players operating in-country. If this were a traditional sales scenario, Mr. Political-Situation would be a classic gatekeeper with veto power. Mr. Political-Situation can keep you from advancing your business.

Even worse, he may allow you to invest money, time, and resources but ultimately not allow you to succeed in any meaningful way. Carefully assess the political situation to determine if it's good for your business or if another country may be better suited to your business success.

If you are considering entry into a country where the political situation is unstable or worsening, it might be advisable to select another country to target so that you can watch the developments and wait out the storm.

Political certainty is difficult to gauge. Consult with the US Embassy; examine trade relations, and read both US and international news feeds. How do you and others that you trust "feel" about the political situation? Evaluate government stability, protocols, decision process, transparency, practices, corruption, and other indicators. Analyze the factors independently and collectively. Intuition is often worth consulting.

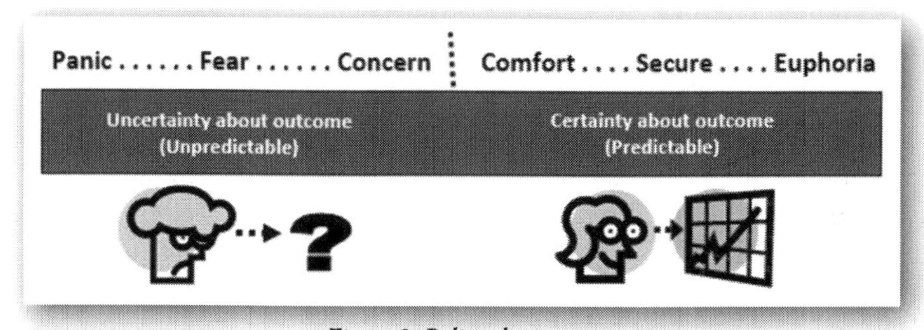

Figure 8: Political certainty

If you are bringing new productivity tools to improve a country's major industries or to leverage natural resources, government support will be a great asset. Government can just as easily stand in your way as help you; it is up to you to approach the government officials involved and build relationships.

Political relations between the United States and your target country won't necessarily be an **accelerator**, but they can open the door for business acceleration under the right set of circumstances.

There is value in shared ethical standards. Look at S. C. Johnson as an example. S. C. Johnson (www.scjohnson.com) is an American manufacturer of household cleaning supplies with sales in 110 countries. The business started with floor wax and today has over thirty-five well-recognized brand-name products, including Drano, Pledge, Saran Wrap, and Windex.

S. C. Johnson has a long company history of building strong relationships with government. In the 1930s, H. F. Johnson Jr. traveled to Brazil to ensure a sustainable supply of carnauba wax for the company's popular products. This resulted in establishing a plantation and, later, factories, which provided jobs and training. The company is committed to building sustainable operations within the countries where it opens factories. The company builds strong relationships with local communities and government. It invests in people and education while establishing workplaces with high levels of integrity.

Today S. C. Johnson continues to maintain strong in-country ties in Brazil, as illustrated by the recognition of "Best Workplace" by the Great Place to Work Institute in Brazil.[17] S. C. Johnson continues to receive help and support of the communities and governments of the seventy-two countries in which it operates. This reduces the risk of entry into new regions and assists the company's success.

There are many great examples of companies—from a broad range of industries—that display strong corporate ethics as a hallmark of their business success. In turn, these ethical standards influence countries, employees, customers, and the company itself, and therefore shareholders and the bottom line. The Ethisphere Institute (www.ethisphere.com) defines, advances, and measures the standards of ethical business practices that fuel corporate character, marketplace trust, and business success. In recent years, companies such as Accenture, Allstate Insurance, Cisco Systems, Intel, John Deere, LinkedIn, Microsoft, Rockwell Collins, and many more have received recognition for corporate ethics and the positive impacts thereof.

Here are some examples of how political, government, and ethical relationships affect your country selection:

* **Business considerations** of the political situation include the following: What will the government position be to your business entry—encouraging, supportive, neutral, unhelpful, or obstructionist? Always be alert to possible corruption, weak legal systems, weak IP (intellectual property) protection, and government hurdles.
* **Customer considerations** of the political situation include the following: How willing are customers to do business with you, a US company: eager, agreeable, reluctant, or unwilling?
* **Travel considerations** of the political situation include personal safety and the ability to move freely about the country, region, or city.
* **Considerations for affordable entry** include fees, time to enter, regulatory requirements, certification, bureaucracy, and red tape.

Communication and Language

Remember this famous line from the movie *Cool Hand Luke*? "What we've got here is a failure to communicate."

The ability to communicate is important to every successful endeavor. Communication is the meaningful exchange of information between two parties: buyer and seller, partners in an agreement, vendor and customer, principal and agent, or even husband and wife.

We know how this works. It's the same in friendships, dating, partnerships, and marriage. When it works, it's great. When it doesn't work, look out! To quote another great film, *Apollo 13,* "Houston we have a problem." Effective communication requires that the sender and receiver convey and interpret the information in the same context.

Typically language is nothing more than a **speed bump**. Language issues scare many companies, and that keeps them from international expansion. Yes, language is a consideration for product markings, documentation, and agreements, but all of those can be addressed.

Communication problems with the use of language can even occur between native speakers of the same language. Take the word "application." In a business meeting, saying something that seems straightforward, like "our innovative application provides this, that, and the other thing," could well end up with some very different interpretations.

Alex, the executive vice president, sent out a meeting invitation to four key TolpaTek directors. Meeting subject: Applications for Singapore. In the meeting notes, he asked each director to come prepared to discuss his or her applications approach for this important new market.

When ten o'clock on Thursday rolled around, everyone assembled in the conference room ready to discuss applications for Singapore.

* *Samir, director of engineering, was eager to begin because the engineering team had been working late, custom configuring application software for Singapore.*

* *Jessica, the IT director, and Michael, director of marketing, were prepared to demo mock-ups of an "app" for the Singapore market. The app would provide system access via mobile devices and could be available in the four official languages of Singapore: Malay, Mandarin, Tamil, and English.*

* *Taylor, the human resources director, had researched local hiring practices and tailored an application form specifically for Singaporean candidates seeking employment with TolpaTek.*

Alex called the meeting to order, thanked everyone for attending, and explained, "We are here to discuss applications for Singapore." Everyone nodded his or her head in agreement, looking at each other with enthusiasm to discuss what each of them had prepared.

Alex continued, "Specifically, we want to address workflow-process design for Singapore." What? Everyone looked at Alex quizzically, and then looked at each other. Were they in the wrong meeting?

They were all prepared to talk about applications for Singapore. But, each had defined "application" completely differently. Samir was prepared to talk about computer software applications. Jessica and Michael had built a mobile app demo. Taylor had brought applications for employment. Yet, Alex wanted to talk about the business application of workflow process. How could this happen?

This is a great example of four correct, yet distinctly different, interpretations of the word "application."

They were all correct in their interpretations, based upon their department's common use and understanding of the word "application." The intended meaning by Alex, the initiator of the business meeting, was something different. It can happen to anyone.

Translation difficulties occur even when using a common language. These will magnify with multiple language interpretations. Plan ahead: skilled translation will be required.

There are 7,106 living languages in use worldwide. Six thousand have registered population numbers, and 560 languages (8 percent) are considered in regular use, according to SIL International. The good news is that you won't need to translate your product interface and supporting documentation into all of them.

English is the language of business in many countries around the world. English is also the primary language spoken by large portions of the population of many countries.

Bringing your United States–based business into a country where English is the predominant language has its advantages. The product and services may be able to enter the target country as is or may require only minor language modification.

Country	Region	Population	English Primary language
United Kingdom	Europe	63,705,000	Yes
Canada	North America	34,880,000	Yes (ex. Quebec)
Australia	Oceania	23,520,299	Yes
Ireland	Europe	4,581,269	Yes
New Zealand	Oceania	4,433,000	Yes
Bahamas	Caribbean	371,960	Yes
United States	North America	318,224,000	Yes

Figure 9: Countries with English as the primary language

There are also many countries where English is not the primary language but is used by much of the population (de facto standard), may be the language of law (de jure), or may co-reside with local languages. These countries may be excellent starting points for expanding into new international markets.

Country	Region	Population	English used in practice
India	Asia	1,247,540,000	Yes
Pakistan	Asia	165,449,000	Yes
Nigeria	Africa	148,093,000	Yes
18 Other African Countries	Africa	128,720,000	Yes
Philippines	Asia	90,457,200	Yes
South Africa	Africa	47,850,700	Yes
Tanzania	Africa	40,454,000	Yes
Kenya	Africa	37,538,000	Yes
Sudan	Africa	31,894,000	Yes
Uganda	Africa	30,884,000	Yes
Papua New Guinea	Oceania	6,331,000	Yes
Singapore	Asia	5,312,400	Yes

Figure 10: Countries with English as de facto standard

Targeting English-speaking countries can be a good business proposition. The top six countries with English as the primary language contributed 33 percent of the world GDP; that contribution grows to more than 38 percent when adding the countries with English as de facto standard.[18]

A discussion of language also brings up the question of product naming and global branding. While English may be the language of international business, it is worthwhile to research product naming and branding in-country. Product names do not need to be the same worldwide, although it can make product identification easier for multinational and global customers. Changing a product name in certain countries or regions may also be helpful, as variations of features, functions, and pricing may be required in different areas.

Another consideration is that your US product or company name may not translate well in another language or another country. The automobile industry has some interesting and humorous examples.

The Chevrolet division of General Motors introduced a compact automobile into the United States in 1962. It was designed to be a straightforward, back-to-basics compact car and came in three models: the Chevy II 100-Series, the Chevy II 300-Series, and the Nova 400-Series. The Nova was the sportiest of the models with a different body design and offering a convertible option. The Nova name and this sporty, affordable compact car were a hit with the US public, connecting to images of novelty and new design or attracting stargazers to the name. No matter what the intent was for the name, by 1969 the Nova name had replaced the Chevy II name.

General Motors routinely marketed their cars outside of the United States, sometimes retaining the same product name. But when GM tried to bring the car into Mexico and other Spanish-speaking countries using the Nova name, the car did not sell well. Upon investigation, GM learned that "no va" means "not going" or "does not go" in Spanish. Fact or urban legend? The dismal sales figures speak for themselves.

The Ford Motor Company has a similar story regarding the Ford Pinto. The Pinto was a subcompact car introduced in the early 1970s. The car featured a sporty two-toned paint job and was named Pinto because it was reminiscent of a horse with distinctive two-color marking we call a pinto or a paint. Ford found that it was unsuccessful at marketing the Pinto in Portuguese-speaking countries like Brazil. Ford learned that "pinto" is a slang term in Portuguese for "small penis." Not surprisingly, few Portuguese men were interested in purchasing the car! Ford renamed the car "Corcel," Portuguese for horse, but it was too late to overcome the naming snafu and other issues.

Here are some impacts of language on your country selection:

* **Customer considerations** of language include training, product markings, product instructions, and product name.

* **Business considerations** of language include workflow, documentation, pricing, packaging, and common courtesy.
* **Travel considerations** of language include navigating taxi service and public transportation.
* **Considerations for affordable entry** into the country include need for interpreters or business/travel guides.

Economic Climate

Key economic trends affecting the prosperity of a country combine to create the economic climate. Instead of temperature, humidity, and wind, economic climate considers patterns in unemployment, exchange rate, inflation, industrial production, income, and other factors.

Typically, the economic climate of a country will be no more than a **speed bump**. But, if you are not aware of the economic trends in-country, you can't take advantage of them or avoid the pitfalls they might present. Economic trends can work in your favor, or they can stall business opportunities.

There are a wide variety of theories and methodologies for measuring or understanding economic patterns; some are very logical and mathematical, while others are not so easy to understand. You don't need to have a degree in economics or be a Harvard PhD. Read local business news feeds for a few weeks, and you will be able to pick up on some of the key economic trends; after a few months, you will have a fairly good picture.

The ideal situation is one in which economic trends are **accelerators**. Most factors of the economy, like currency and exchange rates, will be out of your control. But other aspects of the country's economy may be something your business can leverage for success.

Some economic areas to consider for leverage in-country include

* bringing jobs into a country with high unemployment,
* helping strengthen the industrial production within the country,
* assisting with development of the economy in general, and
* utilizing natural resources to benefit the country or its workforce.

If your assessment is that the economic climate of the country may be a barrier to entry, look for another country to bring your business into. Continue to monitor the economic progress of the country and select a more favorable time to enter—either when your organization has more international experience or is better able to take on the risk.

Currency and exchange rates are something to be aware of. You don't have any control over them, but they are a factor in how you do business. Currency is money (okay, you knew that!). Banknotes, or paper money, are easily exchanged between currencies, but coins are typically only used within a country. The type of currency can provide flexibility, like the euro, which is accepted in eighteen European countries, or currency can be limited to use only within a specific country, like the Thai baht. Currency and exchange rate resources are plentiful. Search for "currency converter" to find many resources, from brand names to new apps.

Exchange rate is the value at which one currency will be exchanged for another. It is an indicator of purchasing power and perception of relative value within a country, which can be translated into that country's ability and willingness to buy your product offering.

The shopping cart. If all products and services were freely traded, an identical shopping cart of products and services would have the same relative value no matter what the currency. Unfortunately, perceived value can vary dramatically depending on the country. Your shopping cart of US products and services, when converted into yuan (or renminbi) will likely be viewed by Chinese buyers as expensive relative to a shopping cart of Chinese products and services. Take that same shopping cart of US products and services to Singapore, and it will likely be viewed as on par or a good value in Singaporean dollars. **Relative value is important in attracting buyers as well as building a profitable business in-country.**

Monetary trends form as exchange rates fluctuate over time. The exchange rate is a snapshot, whereas a monetary trend is more like a movie showing relative changes over time.

If the exchange rate for the US dollar (USD) is dropping, so that it takes more USD to purchase another currency, the dollar is weakening, and the other country's currency is gaining strength. When the dollar loses value, it is cheaper for buyers in-country to purchase your product or service. If you are entering a country where this is the trend, buyers in-country will view this as positive because their purchasing power is increasing. If the dollar is losing value. It's bad news if you haven't planned for it. It is only a speed bump, however, if you have built flexibility and additional margin into your pricing, because the weakening dollar means that you will be receiving less USD over time.

On the flip side, if you are entering a country where the dollar is gaining strength against the local currency, buyers in-country may view this negatively. As buyers are losing purchasing power, the relative value of your offering is perceived as more expensive over time. In these market conditions, the strength of your value proposition is key. If customers perceive the value gap as wide, and your offering is compelling, buyers will continue to purchase. If not, they may choose to look elsewhere or do nothing at all.

Exchange rate is increasing	Stable exchange rates	Exchange rate is dropping
Dollar is gaining strength *Able to buy more local currency*	No change	Dollar is weakening *Able to buy less local currency*
US purchasing power is improving	A strong USD—your goods are relatively costly	US purchasing power is deteriorating
In-country purchasing power is deteriorating	A weak USD—your goods may be affordable	In-country purchasing power is improving
Relative value—US goods are growing more expensive	Relative value remains constant	Relative value—US goods are becoming cheaper
Your in-country price will go up, if it fluctuates with exchange rates	Stable pricing	Your in-country price will go down, if it fluctuates with exchange rates
Your price may have to go up to maintain margin	Stable margin	With no price change, margin % will improve
Build in price flexibility to stabilize prices and maintain buyers		You could reduce price, maintaining % margin, but not USD profit

Figure 11: Effect of exchange rates

Consider the impact of economic climate as you enter a new country:

* How does your pricing in-country compare with similar domestic or imported product offerings?
* Will your product or service offering be able to hold its value, price, and margin as the economic climate changes?
* How will the economic climate affect partners, suppliers, service providers, and other links in your customer chain? Can your company and your ecosystem of partners maintain margin and price performance while building sales volume over time?

Reduce the Customer Risk

There are two critical aspects of reducing the customer risk:

* the risk of being able to attract customers, and
* the risk customers perceive in doing business with you.

The risk of being able to attract customers is finding buyers. Your ability to identify and close the value gap is crucial to reducing your risk of finding buyers. This is a key concept in chapter 2, "Add Value." You must be able to offer, deliver, and create value for your customers.

The risk customers perceive in doing business with you is their willingness and ability to do business with you. Your ability to get traction in-country is vital. Introductions to customers from a trusted mountain guide provide the initial footing. Offering customers proof-of-concept trials can accelerate product popularity and acceptance. These important ingredients of your international strategy are discussed in greater detail in chapters 4 and 5, "Find a Mountain Guide" and "Build Trust."

Buyer Behavior

Your ultimate goal is to have buyers in-country that are willing and able to buy your stuff.

This is Business 101, a sales and marketing basic. Are there in-country customers who want what you are selling and will make a buying decision? Ability *and* willingness to buy combine to establish demand and accelerate sales growth. Without a healthy combination of both, you may close a few deals, but sales will stall because you will be unable to create demand.

Ability to buy: Do buyers have adequate, available funds to purchase your stuff? Do buyers have the authority and access to money necessary to acquire your offering? Ability to buy is affected by business practices in-country. Consumer ability to buy will be affected by access to funds and cultural norms. In many countries business decisions are collaborative, requiring agreement of others. Japan is a good example of decision-making by consensus.

Willingness to buy: Are buyers interested in obtaining your stuff? Will buyers prioritize your stuff above other spending needs? Do buyers perceive that the value in your offering is important enough to create a sense of urgency for them to buy now? Need and willingness to buy can be subjective as customers evaluate perceived value; value can be a matter of individual discretion. Competition will play a role as customers gauge relative value.

Sell to the MAN: Sell to the decision-maker; the MAN could be in the hands of a woman. MAN is an acronym for **M**oney, **A**uthority, and **N**eed. This simple acronym is a straightforward summary of ability and willingness to buy. If any one of these three components is missing, a successful sale is unlikely. Though we couldn't find the source for this well-known acronym, it is familiar to many in sales. Money and authority combine for the ability to buy. Need is the foundation of the willingness.

In addition to ability and willingness to buy, we add the importance of trust—the trust between buyer and seller. Can buyer rely on seller to deliver? Can seller rely on buyer to pay? It may be subjective, but an underlying trust needs to be in place. Focus questions on in-country customer needs. Listening carefully helps new in-country customers build trust that they can rely on you. More on building trust is in chapter 5.

Trust over time is important to both B2C and B2B relationships. Will products and services be accessible in the future? Will products and services maintain the same quality or service over time? If repeat buyers, customer loyalty, or customer relationships are important to your business, trust over time is important. Follow up and follow through in a timely manner to demonstrate that you and your offerings can be trusted in a long-term relationship. This is a business basic. Set an expectation and follow through on time or, better yet, ahead of time.

Confidence is an important outcome of a trusted relationship. Confidence can be a positive preexisting factor, like strong confidence in American products and services. When setting up a new flight operation in Senegal, one company had hired pilots trained in the United States first because they are deeply respected for their knowledge, experience, and safety record. Confidence in working with American pilots was already established. Conversely, uncertainty leads to worry and concern over the risk of failure. There will be prevailing opinions about American industry and doing business with US companies; look to understand these.

Confidence can be further strengthened with customer case studies and third-party evaluations, such as industry articles or analyst validation. Your brand recognition and market share can also boost confidence. As in the United States, a referral or reference from a trusted source is very powerful.

Investment Worthy

What's good for your customer is good for you. Are your goods or services worthy of your customer's investment? Is the market opportunity in-country worthy of your company investment?

Yes, size does matter! Market size is an **accelerator** for your business; many customers prefer to be trending along with other customers making the same smart decisions they are. Customers want to know that you will stick around to serve their needs and that you will continue to invest in their backyard; in-country customers recognize that if their market is investment worthy, you will stick around to support them.

Customers buying a new product just entering their country know that there is an element of risk in doing business with you: you are an unknown to them. Customers want to feel secure that you will be there for them, to both help them get started and to support them in the long haul. When customers see others using your products and services, it's an affirmation of a decision well made. If your product and service offerings include add-ons, additions, or upgrades, customers want the confidence that you will continue to be there when they are ready for the next step.

Entering a new market requires investment of time, resources, and capital. Your company wants to know that the market is worthy of investment and will, over time, produce an appropriate payback. The more potential buyers in-country, the more referrals and references will fuel your business. For both your customers and your company, **it doesn't need to be the biggest market. It needs to be a market that you can penetrate in a meaningful way**.

It is a numbers game. What is the size of *your* market potential? It is not necessarily country size or population. It's who you are selling to. Chile is relatively small in population, but *big* for mining and wine production. Taiwan is a relatively small footprint, but *big* for flexible manufacturing techniques.

Your company is already successful in the United States, so you know what numbers to analyze. They are different for every industry or product. Consumer goods may look for the population of women between fourteen and forty-five, living in urban areas with a certain household income level. B2B tech products may look for companies with fifty or more office workers in a single location. Industrial products may look for manufacturing companies that produce goods that employ aluminum.

The market is different for every product or service offering. You know the characteristics of the market you are looking for. Research the numbers; there are many available sources for market data. Every country has a department of statistics, department of commerce, or department of economic development, which produces market data and makes it available. In specific market segments, industry analysts will also assess and publish market data.

Leverage; don't leapfrog. **Accelerate** to advance; don't hyperextend. Use your company's core competence to maximum advantage. The key features, capabilities, value, and impact you have proven in the United States or other countries are important success levers. Your core strength comes

> from leveraging successful attributes and functions to deliver demonstrable benefit and outcome. Don't forget the power of the Four Whys.

Build a strong confidence base with customers while leveraging your company's core competence. Leverage current product strengths; don't leap into an entirely new product. An entirely new product in a new market brings added cost and risk; your goal is to minimize cost of entry, contain risk, and maximize opportunity. Assess what will need to change in product features and attributes; some will be unimportant to customers in the new country, and new ones may be required. Document your assumptions; develop a matrix comparing known US features, capabilities, value, and impact to those anticipated in the new country you propose to enter.

Do *not* look for Blue Ocean[19] or white space. You are *not* looking for uncontested market space. You are *not* looking to take a new product into a new market; there is too much risk in that. You are looking for a viable market. Sound familiar? We discussed the importance of starting from a position of strength in chapter 2, "Add Value."

Yes, we understand that creating a new market and developing new demand can yield high return. But Blue Ocean, or white space, is *not* our approach to making your first international move or entering a new country. Taking a new product into a new market involves higher product and market risks.

Start with a known and more comfortable position of your current offerings to learn about the new market.

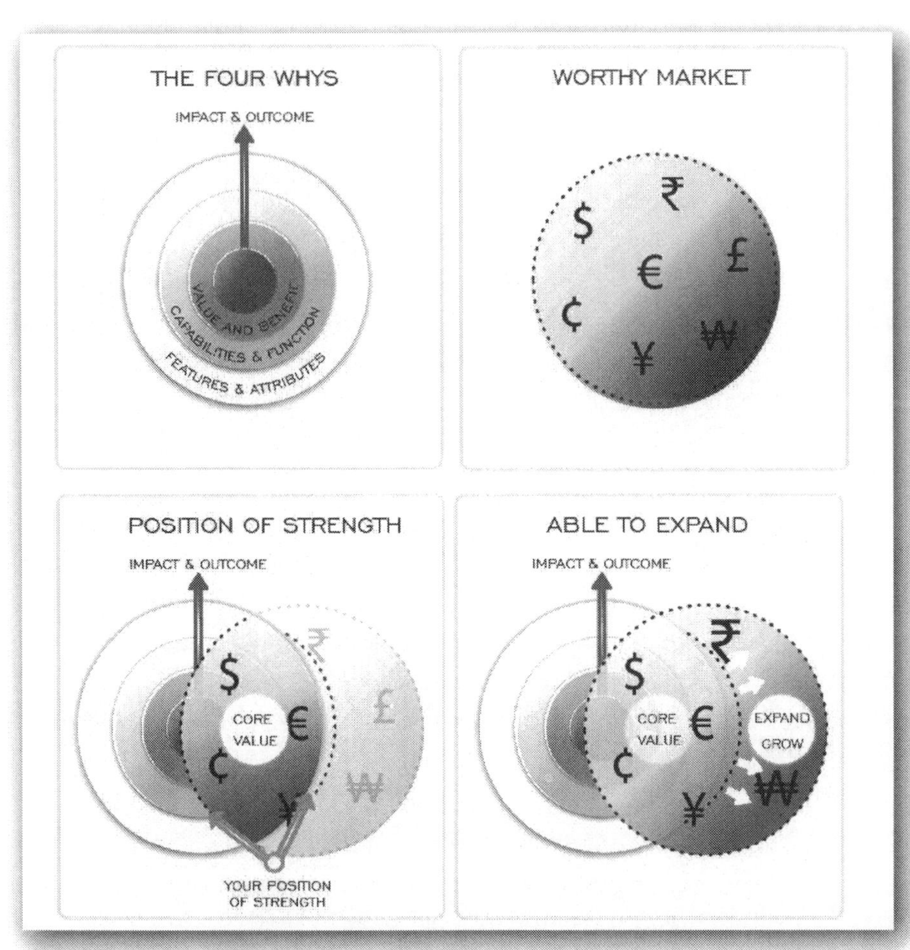

Figure 12: Leverage core value into new countries

Investment worthy is a large enough market size that your company is willing to commit time, money, and human resource to access. Start from a strong confidence base where you can leverage current product features and capabilities and where customers in-country find the value and impact important to them.

Customers willing and able to buy in a new country both expand and diversify your business. "Diversification is a corporate strategy to enter into a new market or industry which the business is not currently in."[20] Entering a new country is a form of diversification.

Product changes may be necessary, but if an entirely new product is required, look elsewhere; find a different country that is better suited for your market debut. There are enough dynamics to deal with in politics, language, business practices, and infrastructure. You already have your hands full as your company needs to acquire new skills, new messaging, and new methodology to successfully open for business in a new country.

Leverage your success in other markets to ripple forward into the new market. If the new market in-country is big enough, the ripples can create waves as your business grows to capture more market share.

Alignment with Business Practices and Culture

What is considered as polite in one country could be an insult in another.

What is expected or required in one country may be unnecessary in another.

A good example of cultural mismatch is the subject of tipping. In the United States, tipping is customary and is expected at restaurants, in taxis, and for many hotel services. Tips of 20 percent for excellent service are common in the United States, with less for good service; leaving no tip is considered insulting, even if the service was poor. In Asia and many Pacific countries, your well-meaning gesture of a tip may be taken as an insult. In Europe, Central America, and South America, many restaurants and hotels add a service charge of 10 percent to the bill, so tipping is unnecessary. In the Middle East and Africa, your tip will not be seen as insulting, but it is probably not required.

Americans afraid to insult others will often tip, no matter what the local customs are. As business has gone more global, this is changing the expectations in many countries. No tipping may be the norm in a country, except when serving Americans. With so many Americans offering tips, local services come to expect it...but, only from Americans.

When planning a business trip to another country, think about the protocols of a typical business day and business week in-country:

Understand how to prepare for the day:

* business attire and
* punctuality expectations for appointments.

Be aware of business etiquette:

* greetings, exchange of business cards, and appropriate forms of address (use of first names, titles, etc.);
* gestures to be understood and gestures to be avoided;
* business gifts; and
* conducting the meeting—agenda flow.

Find out about other business considerations:

* business entertaining and use of alcohol (inappropriate in many countries),
* workday or workweek expectations, and
* holidays or observances.

The religious mix of a country is not directly related to your ability to do business within a country, but it is important to understand. The religious foundation of a country will shape the value system and negotiating style. These can be generalizations, and it is always important to be sensitive to the specific individuals you are working with.

There are numerous sources of information on international business etiquette. Search for general information or country specific, such as "Spanish business etiquette." One of our favorite well-rounded sources is Terri Morrison's classic book *Kiss, Bow, or Shake Hands* and e-learning site (www.kissbowshakehands.com). But even these helpful etiquette tools will not tell you everything, like how deeply to bow, from a simple nod of the head to a full bend at the waist.

A Story over Coffee with Janice Hulse

She had forged a potentially huge multiyear relationship with one of the largest carriers in-country. Now it was time to finalize the commitment at the top of both companies.

Janice Hulse was a senior sales director working for a United States–based unified communications provider. She was introducing the company to new business partners in Japan.

The agreement was signed. Project managers in both companies were appointed. The final step was for a high-level executive meeting. Relationships had been successfully built at the working-levels of the organization. It was important and customary for high-level executives to do the same as a show of respect and mutual commitment.

Janice brought her executive vice president to Japan. The business partner made all the arrangements for a private meeting over dinner in a traditional Japanese tea house. On the evening of the dinner, Janice's EVP announced that he was not feeling up to dinner out and that she could handle it. Janice tried to explain the importance of the meeting, but the EVP just told her, "Handle it." The more she implored, explaining the importance of the meeting, the more annoyed he got. He waved her off. "Janice. Just handle it."

Arriving at the tea house, Janice was impressed with the simple elegance of the historic house, so steeped in tradition that it could date back to the Edo period (circa 1600). The small wooden building was located in a serene manicured garden. Janice entered the welcoming area, where she removed her shoes, stepped onto the tatami mat, and bowed in respectful welcome to her hosts. Seating had been carefully arranged with the highest-ranking executives sitting in the center facing one another. Lesser-ranking officials sat to the left and right.

The business partner executives greeted her and asked when the EVP would arrive. Janice was very polite and regretful, explaining the EVP's absence. She apologized and was quite remorseful. The business partner executives acknowledged this. Then they quietly rose from their seats at the tea table. An executive who sat to the right of the high-level executive approached Janice. He told her that the dinner was cancelled, and with a somewhat stiff move, thrust a gift bag in her direction, instructing her to present it to the EVP. The business partner executives donned their shoes, turned, and left the tea house in silence.

Janice was embarrassed and humiliated. The EVP's absence had been interpreted as a show of disrespect. The business relationship did proceed in accordance with the signed agreement, but the relationship never flourished to the level originally anticipated. It was a painful and expensive lesson in cultural insensitivity.

Learning quickly from experience is a great asset. Janice Hulse's international career continued on a fast track to international vice president of a global multinational corporation and fifteen-plus years' residence in Singapore supporting Southeast Asian customers.

A Social Science Perspective of Cultural Alignment

Alignment with a country culture can help your business thrive. Misalignment can mean failure.

The needs of society are reflected in the cultural values of the country. The concept of "contrasting survival values with self-expression values" is derived from the work of Dr. Ronald Inglehard, Dr. Miguel Basanez, and Dr. Christian Welzel.[21] Survival values are strongest in countries where basic human needs are scarce. Self-expression needs are strongest in affluent countries.

When aligning products and services with a country culture, you will likely find survival values stronger in emerging countries, like those of Africa, whereas self-expression values will be stronger in more advanced countries, like you will find in Europe.

In many emerging countries, attention is on the fundamental needs of society and the basic well-being of the people. In countries such as Bangladesh or Rwanda, import activity is prioritized around subsistence needs: shelter, safety, clean water, food production, waste disposal, electricity, and human health.

✓ If your company's offerings help to elevate the basic needs of a country with strong "survival values" in a cost-effective and manageable way, your products and services will be welcomed.

Advanced countries such as Canada and Ireland have substantially addressed the basic needs of society; they welcome a wide variety of imports that add to the prosperity of individuals and society. Imports that address basic human needs will still be welcome if they bring unique new capabilities and add incremental value. Prosperous and affluent societies, such as Switzerland and New Zealand, look for imports that will expand human creativity; allow for greater self-expression; or address worthy causes such as environmental issues, diversity, sustainability, education, medical research, and conservation.

- ✓ If your offerings promote "self-expression values" in well-off countries, they will be well received.

A company offering a self-contained solar electricity unit could appeal to countries on both ends of the spectrum of survival values versus self-expression values. In areas without power, the solar unit could provide an essential need: electricity. In advanced countries, the solar unit could provide a sustainable and environmentally friendly alternative to fossil fuels.

A simple gravity-fed irrigation system would be very appealing in emerging areas where survival is dependent upon small-plot farmers that grow most of the food. Conversely, this irrigation system would not be a viable business in more affluent, advanced countries.

A health-and-wellness app for smartphones, like the one Kevin McCoy told us about (in chapter 2, "Add Value"), would be appealing in countries with high self-expression values, where the populace is more prosperous and the economy is advanced. The app would not be of interest in countries where survival values are high and basic subsistence needs are unmet.

Figure 13: Fulfilling country survival versus self-expression needs

What is the best alignment for your product or service offering? Are you fulfilling customer needs in areas functioning with scarcity or affluence or something in between?

The work of Dr. Ronald Inglehard also examines another cultural dimension, contrasting traditional religious values with secular-rational values.

The contrasting dimensions of traditional religious values and secular-rational values have multiple facets. Not all elements will affect your business in a new country, but one or more will be important to your customers. We have identified five key elements that may affect your business—progress, methods, perspective, family, and mysticism.

Looking at the central element of progress, countries with more traditional values will hold time-honored practices in high regard, whereas countries with more secular values will appreciate innovative approaches. Methods in a more traditional country may align to an intuitive approach, whereas a more secular country will have greater respect for scientific methods. The "perspective" of a more traditional country may be centered on local and nationalistic values, in contrast to a more secular country's interest in how it fits on the global stage.

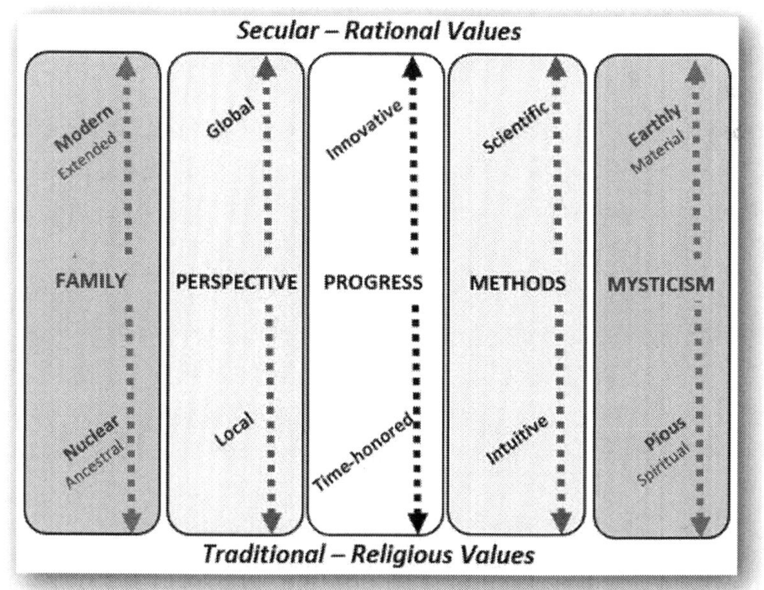

Figure 14: Fulfilling country traditional-religious versus secular-rational needs

These contrasting dimensions of traditional versus secular values are not as straightforward as survival versus self-expression values, but they are no less important.

- ✓ Countries in Latin America and Africa with strong, traditional religious values will typically have people and businesses that value products and services supporting time-honored methods that support their local needs.
- ✓ Countries in Europe, such as Sweden, Norway, and Denmark, with stronger secular-rational values will look for more new, innovative methods that will strengthen their positions on the global stage.

Apply your expertise and industry knowledge to assess how this dimension aligns with your products and services.

Some offerings will align better with one end of the spectrum versus another; others may be "agnostic" and appealing to all. IT infrastructure and system management capabilities with high-end functionality could be highly appealing in countries at both ends of the spectrum. We will hear more about this from Daniel Turner in chapter 5, "Build Trust." Kuwait, a country with largely traditional religious values, wanted the most modern and innovative computing technology globally available when upgrading vital infrastructure.

How does your product or service offering align on the traditional / secular dimension? Are you fulfilling more traditional customer needs or more secular needs? No culture or country fits neatly into any one category, so your evaluation won't be easy. Your assessment will suggest business or population segments that will best fit your offering.

- * A game, activity, or destination resort that promotes family time could have high appeal to those with stronger traditional religious values, in countries such as Russia, Romania, or Bangladesh.

* Smart home devices with entertainment, security, and environmental controls will likely have higher appeal to people, cultures, and countries with more secular-rational values, like Ireland, Australia, or Switzerland.

Let's put these two dimensions together and return to the work of Dr. Inglehard for the social science assessment. Doctors Inglehard, Basanez, Welzel, and others compiled work done by a global network of social scientists, formulated the World Values Survey, and developed the World Values Map[22] pictured below.

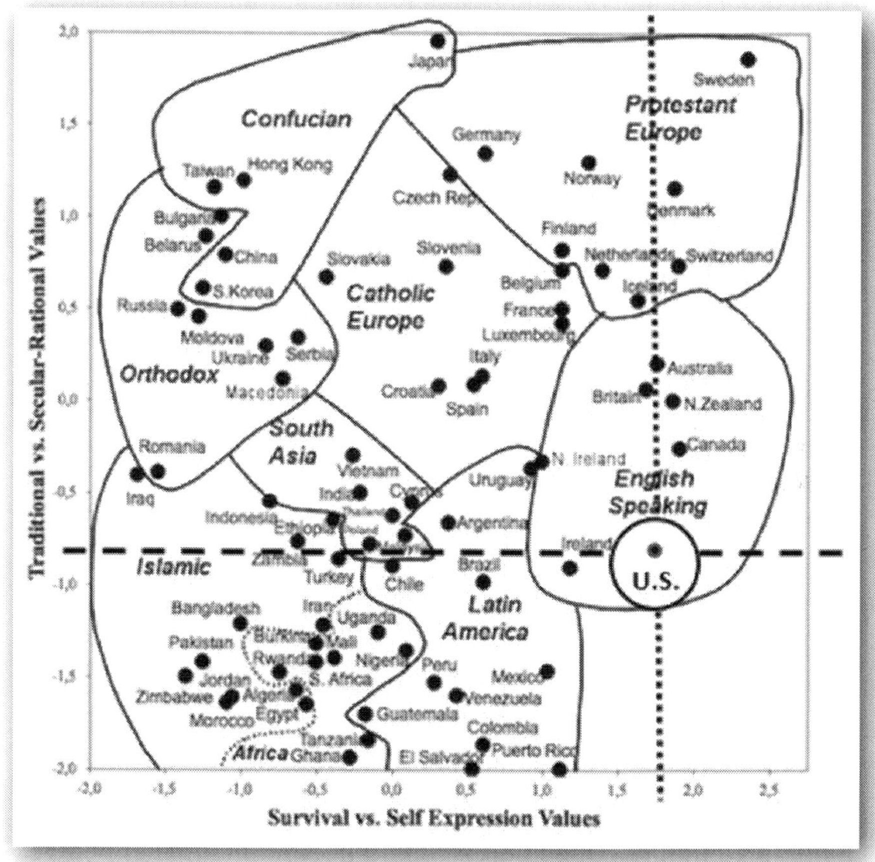

Figure 15: World Values Map

The World Values Survey was designed to provide an integrated measurement of key areas of human concern, from religion to politics and from economic to social life. Their work had a different purpose, but we think it provides interesting clues to which countries might be best for your product and service offerings.

Traditional versus secular-rational values rise on the vertical axis.
Survival versus self-expression span the horizontal axis.

We overlaid two lines on the World Values Map, a horizontal dashed line and a vertical dotted line intersecting the United States. The United States is positioned in the lower right of the World Values Map. This means that the World Values Map situates the United States as more traditional with high self-expression values. Since you have a strong base of experience in the US market, this allows you to assess a country relative to your understanding of the United States.

Above the **horizontal dashed line** of traditional/secular-rational values are countries with stronger secular-rational values than those in the United States. Countries listed on this World Values Map might look for products and services that bring new offerings, new capabilities, and incremental value to users. India would welcome innovative offerings that could expand the industrial sector, which accounts for 26 percent of GDP and employs 22 percent of the workforce,[23] especially in fast-moving consumer goods and agricultural productivity.

Below that same **horizontal dashed line** are countries that will have even stronger traditional values than those of the United States. Products and services that help their national pride or outlook will likely be appealing. This could include products and services that promote (or leverage) a country's natural resources, build a center of excellence in fields unique to the country, or support traditional values. Peru would welcome products and services designed to stimulate manufacturing (22 percent of GDP) or mining industries (15 percent of GDP).

To the **left** of the **vertical dotted line** of survival/self-expression values are countries with more dominant survival values than those of the United States; look far to the left for the countries where the needs are most dramatic. These countries will welcome products and services that enhance survival, safety, clean water, waste disposal, electricity production, health, job creation, and other survival-enhancing offerings. Many countries on the African continent would welcome products and services that elevate basic human needs.

To the **right** of that same **vertical dotted line** through the United States are very few countries. The United States is among a small number of countries with high self-expression values, as assessed by the World Values Map. To these countries, bring products and services that promote environmental protection, human creativity, entertainment, access to information, diversity, or rising demand for participation in decision-making.

It is our opinion that cultural stimulus can be an **accelerator** for your business. Business practices and culture are not within your sphere of influence or control. But there are factors embedded within business practice and culture that you can leverage for success.

Cultural stimulus can simultaneously be a **speed bump** because you need to function cooperatively within the new cultural environment. By doing your homework and working with an in-country representative, your mountain guide, you should be able to comfortably navigate business practices and cultural considerations.

Alignment with a country culture can help your business thrive. Misalignment can mean failure. Here are some ways that business practices and a country's culture might affect your country selection:

* **Customer considerations** of culture help determine the acceptance and impact of your offering for users. You can better consider what will work and what won't work, given cultural considerations. For example, in a Muslim country where most women wear hijabs, hairspray will not be in high demand. Recognition of country culture helps you assess customer readiness and interest for your offering.

* **Business practice considerations** are to work within the country's business cycles, government phases, religious holidays, and family vacations. These considerations should factor into your decision for product-launch timing and the background of your mountain guide. Also consider these factors when deciding which gender would be the best fit for work to be accomplished.

* **Other business considerations** include the perception of corruption within the country. Unequal distribution of power and wealth can lead to perception and practice of corrupt or unethical behavior, which may be very subtle, such as preferential treatment. Or corrupt practices may be very blatant, such as kickbacks, bribes, and payoffs. Transparency International helps provide a relative index at www.transparency.org.

Receptive to American Imports

Balance of trade, import/export activity, and industrial production are indicators of a country's economic health and its citizens' willingness to buy products and services from outside their country. Willingness to buy, discussed earlier in "Buyer Behavior," also includes willingness to buy products and services from the United States. Don't get confused by the flip-flop use of the words "import" and "export." It's all a matter of perspective: who is bringing products in (import) and who is shipping out (export) depends on where you live and work.

TolpaTek wants to leverage all the knowledge and resources that it can get its hands on before making its first move out of the United States and into Canada. Alex approached the US Department of Commerce; he was thrilled and delighted to find a wealth of information. But, he was equally overwhelmed and confused at the vast amount of material. What should be done first? What was critical now versus critical later? Wasn't there some step-by-step formula? How could Alex and TolpaTek tie all the pieces together?

Luckily, Alex came across the International Trade Compliance Institute's (ITCI) "Export Start-Up Kit" and "Trade Information Data

Base" at www.tradecomplianceinstitute.org. It was a breakthrough! This website provided information on the basics of exporting and helped Alex to assess TolpaTek's export potential and readiness. For Alex, it was the step-by-step road map that he was looking for. He told all his business colleagues about it, adding his own humor. He told them, "Finding ITCI was like a GPS for exporting—not a Global Positioning System but a Global Product Selling guide."

The United States is a serious big exporter. Surprised? While it is true that the United States has sent a lot of manufacturing processes offshore, it still has a lot of rockin' products and services that are valued exports. Yes, US imports *do* exceed US exports. *But*, the United States consistently ranks in the top five of world exporters, most years positioned as number three or even number two.[24] In one year alone, American companies export over $2 trillion (yes, trillion with a *T*) in goods and services to more than 150 countries. That includes everything from beverages to toilets, maintenance services to travel, and a staggering list of other offerings you might never imagine as global trade.

Exporting is not exclusive to merchandise, raw materials, and products. Service exports consistently represent about one-third of American exports, and the United States consistently ranks at the top of the list for worldwide service exporters. The services we export include banking, computer services, engineering, express delivery, insurance, legal services, health-care services, tourism, and more.

Despite what you might think, the import/export field is not the sole purview of the big-conglomerate corporate trader. According to the US Department of Commerce (www.commerce.gov), the big guys make up only about 4 percent of all exporters. That means that the other 96 percent are small- to medium-sized companies.

Globalization depends upon international trade and is the foundation for multinational corporations, outsourcing, offshore production, and other well-recognized business practices. Without international trade, countries would be limited to products and services produced within their own countries. There are numerous sources that can help you investigate the balance of trade and industrial production of a country. Here are a few of our favorite sources:

Export.gov (www.export.gov) is a portal partner of the US Department of Commerce that "brings together resources from across the US government to assist American businesses in planning their international sales strategies and succeed in today's global marketplace." We find Export.gov contains lots of good information including export basics and trade problems.

International Trade Association (ITA) is a division of the US Department of Commerce. The vision and mission of ITA is to "foster economic growth and prosperity through global trade" in order to "create prosperity by strengthening the international competitiveness of US industry." The three business units of ITA are: Global Markets, Industry & Analysis, and Enforcement & Compliance. ITA (www.ita.doc.gov) provides lots of information, resources, and services including regional experts, trade promotions, and country-specific export services. The association also has offices around the country.

National Trade Data Bank (NTDB) (www.stat-usa.gov) is another valuable information resource. This is an information aggregator for the government pulling data from multiple sources. NTDB contains information regarding basic export activity, industry-specific information, country-specific information, and industry-country information.

US Department of Commerce (www.commerce.gov) contains a wealth of information. Data are available by NAICS codes (North American Industry Classification System), so you can get industry-specific data. The mission of the Department of Commerce is to "help make American businesses more innovative at home and more competitive abroad."

World Trade Organization (WTO) is a membership organization (www.wto.org) based in Geneva, Switzerland, that deals with the rules of trade between countries. The WTO has about 160 member countries and a wealth of information on each member country, including a straightforward trade profile. WTO updates the trade profiles annually. You will find information including trade topics, documents, data, and resources.

Is the country receptive to US imports? Does the United States have a history of exports to the country you are looking to enter? Existing import relationships can help make your entry into a country easier. There are resources in the United States and in-country that can help you navigate through the process. You can review US export data and trends. Just remember that numbers are indicators and don't tell the real story of penetration, but they will provide a head start to understanding.

If the export/import relationship includes products and services in your industry, it will help to **accelerate** entry. In the export/import world, the trend is your friend. If the United States has a strong, existing export relationship with the country, it will make your entry easier. Fees, regulations, and process will be known and understood, so you don't have to be the pioneer.

If the United States does not have an existing import/export relationship with the country, expect entry to take longer and require greater investment, but, hopefully, it will only be a speed bump, not a barrier to entry.

Import/export questions to consider as you enter a new country include the following:

* What are the import or export restrictions? Countries with fewer restrictions will obviously be easier than ones with greater restrictions.

* Does the country value recognition in international markets?

* Is there domestic production of similar products and services? If yes, how will importing your offering affect the country's domestic business? Does the country import or export products and services similar to those you propose to bring into the country?

Be a De-Risk Detective

A good business person thinks like a detective. Good international business people are investigators that don't miss any detail, whether it is delicately subtle or sternly concrete.

Research is detective work on steroids. The first and most important step in launching your research efforts is to know what you are looking for. What questions are you trying to answer? What supporting data would help you make informed decisions?

There are two types of research: primary and secondary. Primary research is where you gather the data yourself, directly from the source. Secondary research is using data that someone else gathered. Let's start with the second, first—it's at your fingertips.

Secondary Research

Secondary research is summarizing information from existing sources. You will form your own opinion about the material and information you are reviewing, but you are not the source of the data. The Internet is the most powerful form of secondary research because there is an immense amount of information at your fingertips. Other common sources of secondary research are networking, use of industry analysts, market research firms, universities, and trade associations.

A Story over Coffee with Robert Pearlstein
Robert was working on an opportunity where he had identified a unique application for robotics technology in the mining industry. Mining is a big market globally, but not having expertise in this market, Robert was in a quandary as to how to get started. The first thing he did was to contact the US Department of Commerce, which shared lots of information on the global mining sector. He learned that Canada and Australia might be great markets to explore, especially because English is the primary language. Further online research led him to mining industry trade associations where he identified companies that might have interest in this unique application. Then Robert began networking, using LinkedIn to make contact.

Network. Whom do you know with information that can assist your international expansion?

Whom do you know from the target country? It could be someone working in your company, a network contact, or a friend of a friend. Someone who has recently moved or immigrated to the United States from the country you are looking to enter can be a great help. This person can tell you about local customs and some details of life that are not readily available. His or her information will be subjective, but it can provide a view of everyday life in-country.

If your network contact is within your company or industry, he or she can provide you with relevant business information and contacts. Check your LinkedIn and Facebook networks for people who include location information for past employers, college(s) attended, and languages spoken. This can clue you in to people in your network who are from a specific country. People love talking about their home country and will answer questions endlessly on any topic both big and small.

Within your company are tremendous resources ready to help. The marketing department will know relevant sources of market data and have access to them. The engineering department may be able to provide technical information regarding power requirements, system interfaces, and other relevant operational intelligence. Finance will help with financial transactions, legal requirements, agreements, and other critical business factors. Human resources will be helpful later on and supply information regarding hiring practices in other countries. Build an internal team to help you find the information you need; read more on that in chapter 5, "Build Trust."

Industry Analysts and Market Research Firms. These are both expert suppliers of information. They typically perform both primary and secondary research to produce industry reports. There are many well-respected firms that are considered to provide authoritative opinions and are trusted within their industry for assessments and projections. Using their depth of industry expertise and experience, these firms will segment industry markets, forecast growth or changes, size market segments, and rate players within the market.

Industry reports can be worth paying for. Evaluate your needs and what questions you are trying to answer so that you can select the right report or set of reports that will suit your needs.

There are many industry analysts and market research firms to pick from; your company will already have a relationship with one or more. Leverage current analyst relationships to find the specific reports that will help you in your country selection and in-country product launch. Many of these firms also stage annual events that could be great for networking, making connections, and broadening your knowledge.

Here are names of a few industry analysts and market research firms that Janet and Robert have worked with in the past:

* Computer Review
* Digital Clarity Group
* Forrester Research
* Gartner Group
* IDC (International Data Corporation)
* Lux Research

* McKinsey & Company
* Ovum Ltd.
* Yankee Group

Academics. College and universities that provide degrees, expertise, or specialization in your industry are tremendous resources. This may not seem obvious at first. Colleges and universities look for opportunities to create dialog, liaisons, and partnerships in the industry. The school does not have to be near the headquarters of your business, but if it is nearby, that can benefit both your company and the college or university.

Start with an informational interview with the college or university. You will want to assess mutual objectives and how they intersect to satisfy both your company and the learning institution. Come prepared with information that you are looking to explore. Even in the interview process, expect to gain some interesting insights. Additionally, come prepared to share information. When reciprocal benefits are obvious, a strong relationship can be forged.

Consider the use of interns. If the college or university has students enrolled from the country that you are targeting, your company could employ them as interns. They speak the language and will understand the nuances of getting appointments and communicating value. The benefit to the interns is that they build US industry expertise and business contacts.

There are many different types of internships. Work-experience internships are typically for undergrad students and commonly occur during the summer school break. Research/dissertation internships are typically done by graduate students. Grad students will want research topics that complement their master's or doctoral thesis. If your business is near the college or university, internships can occur during the regular school year, as students will work around their class schedule to fulfill the internship requirements.

A college or university relationship can develop into bigger opportunities for your company. These schools can also produce high-potential new-grad hires.

Trade Associations or Industry Trade Groups. These are an underutilized resource. Although there may be numerous other objectives stated in the organizational charter, the true purpose of trade associations is education, political lobbying, and standardization. Trade associations in the United States are typically nonprofit organizations that are funded by membership from individuals or businesses within the industry sector.

Trade associations will publish considerable information about their industry sector, trends, current issues, and regulatory requirements. Trade associations hold regular member meetings and will typically hold events for members and businesses within the industry. This is a great resource for both information and contacts that may become business partners or customers. Trade associations have websites, publish newsletters or magazines, and may offer member directories; these are a significant source of industry contacts for partners or customers.

A United States-based trade association may have contacts with similar international associations to help open doors for you. Otherwise, feel free to contact an in-country trade association directly. It is helpful to have introductions made by local contacts who speak the local language, as in-country trade associations will have the goal of promoting local business and may not be accustomed to operating in English.

Someone within your company will be a member of an applicable trade association. Engineering, manufacturing, customer service, or marketing will likely already know of relevant trade associations and subscribe to one of their publications, lovingly called "trade rags." Leverage those internal opinions and contacts into trade associations to see if they can steer you toward some in-country contacts. Many trade associations offer educational webinars that might be of interest or hold events that could be useful.

Internet Research. The most powerful secondary research tool on the planet is in your hands, and it doesn't cost a penny, centavo, pfennig, or pin-gin (except for internet access). The primary cost is time, which could be your evenings and weekends; a colleague's time; or the time of an intern, consultant, or market researcher. Whichever way you chose to spend secondary research time, it is time well spent!

If you are doing market research to help you uncover value (chapter 2) look for industry-related press articles and blogs, spend time on competitor websites, and pull competitors' SEC filings (Securities and Exchange Commission filings, which include 10Q, 10K, annual report, and quarterly reports).

Have you ever wondered how competitors have been so successful with their online marketing campaigns? There are online tools for that too, like SpyFu.com. SpyFu.com exposes the search-engine marketing secrets of companies such as keywords, Adwords, and ranking.

Get introduced to the tools available from your favorite search engine. Many tools are free, and others require subscription. Every search engine offers a suite of tools and capabilities: Google, Bing, Yahoo!, Ask, AOL, WOW, Webcrawler, and others.

Amazing possibilities and an incredible amount of information are just a click away.

Primary Research

If you are in sales or marketing, your professional success is based on primary research. You like to talk to people, right? If so, you are skilled in primary research! Primary research is based on direct communication or observation of customers, potential customers, and others involved in the role of buying and using your products or services.

One-on-One Interviews. Talking directly with customers and potential customers provides invaluable information. There is a personal connection made between the interviewer and interviewee with the goal of understanding the interviewee's perspective. In primary research, one-on-one interviews are considered to be qualitative research because the sample sizes are small and focus on the "why" and "how" of decision-making.

The most common forms of business-related interviews fall into two categories: guided interviews and fixed-response interviews. Guided interviews have a preselected set of questions designed to gather the same general information from all interviewees. Guided interviews allow for a degree of conversation and open discussion. Fixed-response interviews ask the same question to all interviewees, having them choose a response from a fixed list of options. Fixed-response interviews limit conversation but make it easier to build statistical data.

Guided interviews can provide a broad range of information. Fixed-response interviews provide responses that can be quantified. Robert and Janet prefer to use a blend of guided and fixed-response questions when doing one-on-one interviews for primary research.

One-on-one interviewing can be done by you, a small consulting company, or a major market-research firm, based on sample size, sophistication, and budget. Technology and social media have sped up one-on-one interviewing. Retail companies will do shop-alongs, use eye-tracking technology, or store flow monitoring. In both B2B and B2C, journal mapping or digital diaries are useful for certain types of products and services.

Focus Groups. The use of focus groups in primary research is mainly reserved for consumer products, but such groups can also be useful to gather input from users and administrators of B2B products or services. A focus group assembles a small number of people, who are asked to share their perceptions, attitudes, and opinions about a product or service. The focus group may be given a presentation or a demonstration or may be allowed to interact directly with the product offering. Using focus groups is considered to be qualitative research.

Focus groups can be conducted face-to-face or online via telephone or web conference. There is a lot of debate about the effectiveness of focus groups because they are often conducted in more laboratory-like settings or are too controlled.

They do provide important qualitative information and can be useful especially as the group members discuss key business topics among themselves.

Our experience with B2B tech products is that focus groups are widely used, but they are not called that. User groups, customer advisory boards, and online communities are forms of B2B focus groups. A degree of industry or product knowledge is required, so focus group activities have a more targeted audience, and companies generally are seeking more specific input.

Surveys. Surveys are the principal source of quantitative research. The sample size needs to be large enough to extrapolate responses representative of a segment of the population. Surveys typically include a structured set of questions with fixed responses. Opinion polls and government census data are good examples. Online tools and social media have revolutionized and simplified the methodology behind survey delivery, data collection, and reporting.

We love all the online tools available today. Small surveys can be conducted quickly within social applications such as LinkedIn, Facebook, and Twitter. The results will reflect the opinions of app users, which may or may not be extensible to nonsocial users. DIY (do-it-yourself) survey tools let organizations prepare and circulate surveys quickly to a captive audience like employees, customers, partners, or purchased lists. We have successfully used DIY survey tools such as Survey Monkey and Zoomerang, and there are many others available as well.

DUH!—Fundamentals Worth Knowing

The simple stuff is helpful, fosters ease of entry, and helps avoid naïve, often costly mistakes. Sometimes the simplest things cause the biggest headaches. The wrong power adapter means that the electronic toys you brought are soon rendered useless because they can't be plugged in or recharged. The killer software can't be demonstrated because the country uses a different operating system. Anticipate potential problems and come prepared, and it will save you unnecessary stress, frustration, and cost. See appendix 3, "Fundamentals Worth Knowing," for additional detail.

Fundamentals and infrastructure should be nothing more than minor **speed bumps**, if you do your homework.

Here are some considerations important to country selection when investigating fundamentals and infrastructure:

* **Customer considerations.** How will your offering work within the country's existing workflow? Will this make efficient use of its current fundamental and infrastructure setup? What changes will customers need to make to accommodate your product offering? Is the need for your product offering great enough so that customers will prioritize needed infrastructure changes to accommodate it?

* **Representative and business partner considerations.** What modifications are required for your offering to perform optimally in-country? Consider performance for partners, suppliers, service providers, and other vendors that will interact with your offering. If change is required in *your* offering, investigate and plan for this in advance. If change is required in the infrastructure of the country, it might be more prudent for you to consider launching your business in another country first.

* **Considerations for affordable entry into a country.** These are a matter of preplanning. Consider all the infrastructure needs of your offering for delivery and use within the country; this will allow you to estimate costs in advance to make the most prudent decisions, with last minute scrambling in-country, costs can quickly get out of control.

Less Is More—Avoid Analysis Paralysis

What you know. What you don't know. What you don't need to know...at least not at first.

"*You've got to be kidding. How am I supposed to know what I don't know?*" Be the detective. What you don't know can be gleaned from reading between the lines of what you do know. Be your own Sherlock Holmes. Once you have collected and written down what you *do* know, go back and look at it again through different lenses. Read between the lines. Look through the lens of a user. Peer at the information from the prospective of the buyer, who may not be the user. How would your in-country representative view what you know, and what other questions would he or she ask?

Talk with people in your personal and professional network to help uncover what you don't know. Our favorite approach is to meet with people for a cup of coffee, as you may have guessed. The small investment of coffee and an hour of time can have enormous payback. We love catching up, looking back, and envisioning ahead with people who have taken a company or product offering into international markets or the specific country we are interested in. It's surprising how fast an hour will zip by and how much incredible insight you will gain. Our favorite "coffee questions" are simple:

* Tell me your favorite "war story" about when you took your product offering into a new international market.
* What do you wish you would have known before you went in-country?
* Even with all your prior knowledge, what were some of the unexpected "gotchas"?
* Where did you waste the most time?

As you have no doubt noticed, we've included a few great stories that we have heard from friends and colleagues over coffee or tea. It can even be a virtual cup of coffee or tea with colleagues who are across the country or across the globe.

Build a file. Collect data and sources. Record your assumptions; don't try to keep it all in your head. Trust us; even the best memory system—whether human or machine—becomes fallible over time. Writing something down requires a level of commitment. It doesn't really matter how you record the data; just find a way that works for you, and **do it**. You can update your files as your knowledge increases and you validate assumptions. Additionally, your knowledge can be more easily shared with others if it's written down.

What you don't need is excessive detail. Don't get bogged down. Don't get trapped in "analysis paralysis." Sure, your boss will always ask one more question than you have the answer to—expect it, but don't sweat it.

The real challenge that you will be faced with is **the dilemma of having too much general data and too little specific information**. There is a plethora of general data available. Look for information specific to your prospective country and your industry segment. *Ignore the rest.*

How to look for information is covered in "Be a De-Risk Detective." We are not trying to turn you into a market research expert, just providing you with useful options to consider.

Who will do the research is a question that only you can answer. It will likely be a combination of effort. You will do more of what you are already doing—Internet research and meeting with people. Your home team will do research, as well as open doors to industry analysts, market research firms, and trade associations. As support for your international efforts grows, you will likely employ an outside consultant, research firm, or an intern to take the research to the next level.

What to look for is important to identifying value (chapter 2) and de-risking the opportunity (chapter 3).

Where to look is everywhere! Check out appendix 1, "Resources & References," for a head start on places to look. New tools and resources become available every day, so continue doing your own research.

Why is so that you make informed decisions. If critical information can be triangulated and verified against two or more sources, you will be confident that your decision is based upon solid data. If information is qualitative or there is only one source, accuracy is uncertain.

Assess Your Risks

Risk assessment can make the difference between success and failure. Risk assessment can make the difference between a safe move into a new country and a hazardous one. Assess your risk, then ask a few other key players in the company to do the same, and compare notes.

① Leverage Assessment

More leverage = less risk

1. Is your company currently selling outside the United States? ☐ NO ☐ YES!
   * If yes, list all the countries.
   * For each country note how long you have been selling in-country and current sales volume. Finance should be able to supply this information.
   * Include US market data for comparison.

2. What country or countries are you targeting for entry?
   * List each target country, anticipated date of entry, and expected sales volume.

3. What leverage exists between your current business (number 1 above) and your proposed international expansion (number 2 above)?

   Assess the strength of leverage by evaluating the parallel to your current operations. Yes answers put you in a stronger leverage position than no answers.
   * Is it an existing product?
   * Are the customer needs the same?
   * Can you use current language for documentation and product markings?
   * Is the currency currently being handled by finance?
   * Is the country adjacent or is geography easily accessible?

② Political Compatibility

This is one area that can be a showstopper. Assess the political compatibility, then ask a trusted executive or board member to do the same, and compare notes.

1. Political climate of current US government relations with the target country?

   ☐ Strong ally ☐ Friendly ☐ Cordial ☐ Tolerant ☐ Weak (enemy)
   Clear skies - Sunny --- Overcast - Dark & Stormy

2. Outlook for current US government relations with the target country?

   ☐ Stable ☐ Improving ☐ Uncertain ☐ Deteriorating ☐ Critical

3. Anticipated position of government in-country?

   ☐ Helpful ☐ Supportive ☐ Neutral ☐ Unhelpful ☐ Opposing
   Describe why. What government initiatives or policies are in place that support your point of view?

4. What ministry, bureau, department, or agency is responsible for handling your industry, products, or services?

5. Anticipated government corruption in-country? Compare your perspective to the "Corruption Perception Index" from Transparency International (www.transparency.org).

   ☐ Little to no corruption ☐ Minor petty corruption
   ☐ Systemic corruption

6. What is the US export activity into the target country?
   * Overall, total US exports to select country
   * Your industry-related US exports into the country
   * Specific US products or competitors' exports

③ Economic Issues

Many economic factors are outside of your control. Leverage factors that work in your favor and develop contingency plans to minimize impact of negative factors. Assess economic issues, ask a trusted executive in finance to do the same, and then compare notes.

1. What are the monetary trends in-country as the exchange rates of the country's currency fluctuate over time? One of the columns in the table below will apply.

2.

Exchange rate is increasing	Stable exchange rates	Exchange rate is dropping
Dollar is gaining strength *Able to buy more local currency*	No change	Dollar is weakening *Able to buy less local currency*
US purchasing power is improving	A strong USD—your goods are relatively costly	US purchasing power is deteriorating
In-country purchasing power is deteriorating	A weak USD—your goods may be affordable	In-country purchasing power is improving
Relative value—US goods are growing more expensive	Relative value remains constant	Relative value—US goods are becoming cheaper
Your in-country price will go up, if it fluctuates with exchange rates	Stable pricing	Your in-country price will go down, if it fluctuates with exchange rates
Your price may have to go up to maintain margin	Stable margin	With no price change, margin % will improve
Build in price flexibility to stabilize prices and maintain buyers		You could reduce price, maintaining % margin, but not USD profit

What stage of economic development is the country considered to be in (chapter 2)?

☐ Advanced ☐ Developing ☐ Emerging

3. How does pricing of in-country competitors compare to your pricing? List the top three competitors, which could be alternatives that are not equivalent to yours. Is their in-country pricing higher, equivalent, or lower than yours? What will be your market strategy? Competition was also discussed in chapter 2 because you want to stand out in the crowd as you deliver value for customers in the new market.

* Competitor 1:
* Competitor 2:
* Competitor 3:

4. Your product may have positive economic impact for the country you are entering. Check all that apply to your offering and with a verifiable measureable impact.

- ☐ Addresses vital substructure for human existence (food production, clean water, air quality, clothing, housing, other).
- ☐ Tackles fundamental infrastructure issues (waste disposal, electricity production, transportation, education, health care, personal safety, other).
- ☐ Addresses safety concerns (crime, terrorism, violence, abuse, other).

• • •

- ☐ Enhances environmental protection.
- ☐ Promotes human creativity, entertainment and self-expression.
- ☐ Increases access to information or participation in decision-making.
- ☐ Promotes tolerance for diversity.

• • •

- ☐ Creates jobs.
- ☐ Builds or creates skills.
- ☐ Strengthens industrial production.
- ☐ Helps in-country business be more competitive locally, regionally, or globally.

Stage of Economic Development Assessment: The first grouping applies to emerging countries or rural, undeveloped areas of countries in other stages of economic development. The second grouping will be important to buyers and users in advanced countries, although they may be needed in less developed countries. The third grouping will be important to any country, in any stage of economic development.

Networking Assessment: For items ticked in the first and third groupings, the country will have a government ministry, bureau, department, or agency responsible and interested in what you have to offer.

④ Language Challenges

Typically language is low risk and nothing more than a speed bump, but it needs to be considered early in the planning process.

1. What language or languages are used in-country?

   * Predominant language spoken: ______________________________

   * Other languages spoken: ______________________________
     ____

   * Predominant language of business: ______________________________

2. For use of your product or service, where is language (written or spoken) critical to deployment, use, or operation? Which areas of language interaction are mandatory, helpful, optional, or not required?

   * documentation
   * packaging
   * use/operation
   * training
   * product markings
   * servicing

⑤ Market Assessment

No buyers = no customers = no business

Assess the market, ask a trusted marketing executive to do the same, and then compare notes.

1. Rate your understanding of buyer behavior and your access to the MAN (money/authority/need). Your assessment can be based on your depth of understanding, or it could be based on the degree of parallel to current operations.

    * ability to buy (access to capital)
    * authority to buy
    * access to decision-makers
    * willingness to buy (need)
    * buyers' sense of urgency

2. Total number of in-country customers that fit your ideal buyer profile. A little Internet research, your mountain guide, or marketing should be able to help you with this.

3. Expected (or desired) percent of market-share capture:

    * Year 1: ________ * Year 2: ________ * Year 3: ________

4. Customer capture. Put the math together from questions 2 and 3 above.
   >>Secret weapon. A spreadsheet will make this a whole lot easier<<

    Number of in-country customers **x** percent market share = customer capture

5. Top-line revenue projection. Take expected average sale per customer, multiply that by your expected customer capture, and you will get a

first cut at expected top-line revenue, if you are selling direct. If you are selling through channels, you will have to adjust this for channel partner margins (distributor, reseller, retailer, etc.).

6. Get that spreadsheet fired up and keep working the numbers. Estimate the following:

   * initial purchase (first year)
   * future purchase potential: subscription, repeat, add-on, upgrade
   * customer retention rate
   * business growth over time
   * and more!

Chapter 4

Find a Mountain Guide

How can friends and neighbors seem so similar and compatible yet be so very different?

TolpaTek ran into one speed bump after another as it began doing business in Canada. The sales cycle was longer. Canadians were more conservative and nationalistic in their decision-making, exploring Canadian alternatives first and carefully assessing comparative value. Canada was more advanced in its licensing agreements and more tightly regulated in other aspects of its financial and commercials systems.

When initially entering Canada, TolpaTek had not quite sharpened its cultural sensitivity skills and began doing business as if Canada were the fifty-first state. Yes, there were cultural similarities. Yes, they spoke English. No, Canada as ***not*** *the United States.*

A breakthrough came when TolpaTek found Samantha Tremblay, a Canadian consultant, who became their in-country mountain guide. Samantha was instrumental in introducing TolpaTek to the right people, the right customers, and the right way to do business in Canada. She made it clear that TolpaTek would not be doing business in Quebec (the second largest Canadian province) or with any government-related entity unless employees could conduct business in French. Canada is a proud sovereign nation, and there are ***two*** *national languages: English* ***and*** *French.*

Canada is slightly larger in land mass than the United States, yet its population is slightly smaller than that of the state of California. Although it was a viable strategy to begin doing business in provinces other than Quebec, Samantha helped TolpaTek build a road map to embrace French to open up all of Canada to its value proposition.

Samantha was TolpaTek's Canadian mountain guide. She helped TolpaTek follow the language requirements of the Charter of the French Language, which makes French the usual language of business in Quebec. She was TolpaTek's navigator for Canadian rules of businesses, employees, products, packaging, advertising, and information technology. Samantha extended her role as mountain guide over the years, helping TolpaTek navigate the labor laws that varied from province to province, as the company hired full-time local Canadian talent.

If you want to climb Mount Kilimanjaro in Tanzania, Pico Bolivar in Venezuela, or Mount Tolpagorni in Sweden, look for a mountain guide who knows *that specific* mountain very well and can lead your team on a safe journey.

Your mountain guide is the navigator for a safe and successful journey. The mountain guide helps you prepare for the trip, plans the route, ensures that proper paperwork is in place, and provides guidance while you are underway. Once you arrive at the airport, your mountain guide greets you and guides the venture. Yes, you are an active participant. *However*, your mountain guide influences your steps to ensure a successful venture and reduces risks with her or his deep knowledge of the mountain.

Your mountain guide is the star starting player in-country. **The mountain guide is an established individual or organization residing in-country,**

speaking the local language, and having deep relevant business experience. The mountain guide is an ambassador—your initial door opener—and will assist in launching your efforts.

Every business has a mountain to climb, first in its home country and later in other countries as its business expands. Maybe TolpaTek recognized this and named their company after beautiful Mount Tolpagorni in the Kebnekaise area of Swedish Lapland.

Why You Need a Mountain Guide

Another Story over Coffee with Andrew Cadwell

"You need to understand the landscape, understand the risks, and speak their language. If you do all of that, you build trust with the clients, and they take you in as one of their own." Andrew Cadwell, division president of a managed IT solutions and network services company, recognized that opening a new market sector has many of the same challenges as opening a new international market.

Industry experience with relevant technology offerings was Andy's top selection criteria for a mountain guide. Andy hired an industry veteran who was able to guide the company in learning how to speak about the solution and who provided credibility in the space. The company was experienced in providing complex solutions in other industry sectors but not in health care.

The mountain guide was essential to Andy, building a three-cornered "wedge" strategy for the health-care industry: 1) add value, 2) walk the talk, and 3) prove the solution.

- *Andy's company added value by helping health-care institutions improve Core Scores to recover more government and insurance reimbursements.*

* *The company walked the talk of a hospital: improving nurse response times, hospital quiet hours, patient readmissions, and more.*
* *It proved the solution by running small proof-of-concept (PoC) installations.*

Andy's mountain guide was vital in translating off-the-shelf technology into health-care-specific value. It's not a one-size-fits-all world in any industry. The mountain guide intimately understood the power of upgrading hospital operations through improved reimbursements and better worker/patient user experience.

With the help of an industry-veteran mountain guide, Andy Cadwell's company started small, became an expert in one significant area, built expertise, and grew into a major industry player. His company was invited to participate in bigger and bigger opportunities.

Your company has spent years finding and building trusted relationships with customers and industry partners in the United States. Now you are looking to do business outside of the United States or in a new industry sector. For some unknown reason, senior management (and maybe even you), think that you can do this on your own. *You can't.* It requires in-country (or in-industry) assistance, and it will take time.

Networking is critical to doing business in the United States—networking connects the dots between trusted relationships. Trust is extended through people in your network to others in their network. Networking works the same way internationally, and **international networking is even more important** than it is within the United States.

Your mountain guide **accelerates** the network process by extending trust in-country through his or her relationships with partners, customers, government, and industry. In the United States, trust can be established fairly quickly, and business relationships will remain intact until proven otherwise. Overseas, trust is built more slowly and cured over time. Your mountain guide helps to build and maintain consistent, respectful communications and therefore trust.

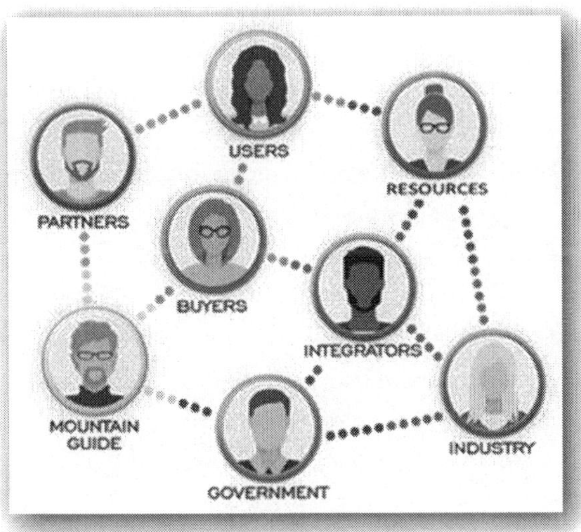

Figure 16: Networking

International business has a sense of urgency, but it's not rushed or pushy. Lots of work can be accomplished via Skype, Google Hangout, or WebEx, but it will not replace the importance of the in-person, face-to-face contact. A proper kiss on both cheeks in France, a kiss on one cheek in Chile, or a bow in Japan just cannot be done remotely.

The local mountain guide helps to maintain person-to-person contact during the time that you are attending to business in the United States and other parts of the world. E-mail and text communications keep things moving but may go unanswered without the in-person assistance of your mountain guide establishing a sense of priority.

A Mountain Guide Benefits Your Company

Use a mountain guide, rather than company employees, early in the entry of a new country to help you understand and better navigate local challenges.

A mountain guide benefits your business and will help you with a vast number of things:

* The guide can help with getting started and opening doors by
  * setting up meetings with influential leaders in industry and business,
  * offering suggestions to configure or customize offerings for his or her country, and
  * explaining collateral needs to be localized and what can remain in English.

* The mountain guide can help develop your business and build your value proposition due to his or her
  * deep understanding of distinctive characteristics of in-country customers, both buyers and users;
  * deep understanding of other partners needed for your in-country business, such as suppliers and distributions channels;
  * relationships with government ministries and agencies for approvals and endorsements; and
  * ability to deal with local laws and customs.

* The guide can help with evolving your business and accelerating trust by
  * maintaining and nurturing in-country relationships and
  * recommending and opening new market segments.

Expect a **bumpy road** when entering a new market. For the many valuable things that a mountain guide will do for you, never lose sight of the fact that his or her main function is to find local "best-fit" customers. Without customers, you do not have a business, and you have not successfully entered that new market.

Local users of a product may be quite different from those in the United States. Your mountain guide will help you identify "best-fit" in-country customers. For example, you may be selling communication equipment to the police in the United States. A good mountain guide from Chile will point out that the best-fit customers are the coast guard and the navy, since the country has a long coastline and these services are responsible for all police activity offshore and ten kilometers inland from the shore.

In addition to helping sell to obvious customers, a good mountain guide will be able to identify other good-fit customers and country-specific opportunities. For example, a company that manufactures walk-through metal detectors for airport security hired a mountain guide in Mexico who introduced them to a large banking company that wanted to use the detectors at the entrances to its banks.

What Mountain to Climb?

If you are climbing Kilimanjaro in Tanzania, a mountain guide from Mount Fuji will not have the right expertise. You want a mountain guide with the right experience.

Before beginning your search, decide what role the mountain guide will fill. If you are dealing with an array of different products or highly varied customer profiles, you may need more than one mountain guide, each with a unique focus. The more the merrier, but know that more management attention and oversight will be required.

Your mountain guide is the key to unlocking an in-country network and maintaining the trusted in-person working relationship when you are not there. In order to fulfill his or her role, the mountain guide must have the necessary action orientation and ability to influence.

The Mountain Guide's Role

Think about your US business today: Where do "partners" fill an important need or function to complete the offering for the ultimate buyer or user?

Start by examining the partners you have in the United States today. If your company sells through channels, distributors, or resellers, you will want a mountain guide with sales and distribution skills. Your mountain guide may actually be the in-country channel or distribution partner.

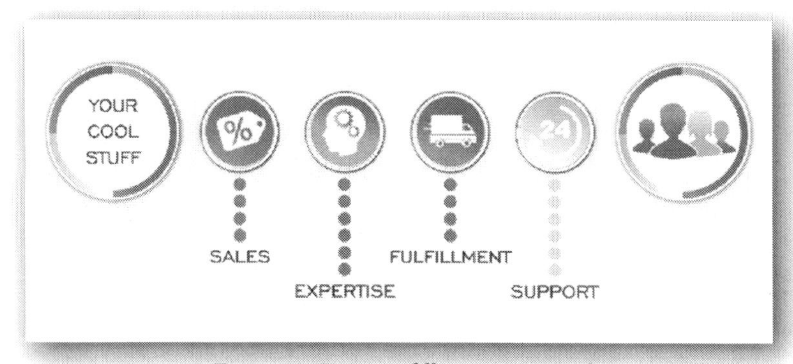

Figure 17: Partners fill important need

OOPS! You don't work with partners in the United States today? Look a bit more closely. Few companies today are completely vertically integrated, performing every function to bring their product to market themselves. Companies outsource certain functions or aspects of the relationship between their offerings and the buyers or users. You may use a telemarketing firm for lead generation, subcontract certain work, hire technical experts as needed, or use a third-party logistics firm. These are examples of partners, even though you may not call them that. You may want your mountain guide to provide a similar function or build similar relationships in-country.

Identify the role your mountain guide needs to furnish. A mountain guide is your partner in-country to connect your offering with customers, buyers, and users. The four main roles or connection points to connect your offer with customers are sales, expertise, fulfillment, and support:

* Sales
    * demand creation and lead generation
    * developing and closing deals

  * on-going customer relationships
  * market access—industry, geography, or something else

* Expertise
  * technical skills
  * industry-specific knowledge
  * system Integration
  * localization

* Fulfillment
  * retail display or demonstration capabilities
  * inventory or delivery
  * installation, implementation, or training

* Support
  * maintenance, repair, or service
  * on-going customer relationships
  * specific technical skills
  * geographic coverage

Action Orientation

Based on the role your mountain guide fulfills, make sure that you are satisfied that his or her action orientation will achieve your desired objectives.

Proactive mountain guides will initiate and drive action with measureable results. Sales is a classic proactive role: finding prospects and developing and closing deals. Our experience is that most companies need proactive mountain guides, especially at initial country entry. Retail requires many proactive functions, such as product display, demonstration, and inventory management, which are necessary for a successful consumer experience. Some industries and products require proactive support for preventive maintenance or sustaining engineering; this is common for some industrial equipment and monitoring centers, for example.

Active mountain guides rely on the performance of other functions to deliver measureable results. For many businesses, an active sales or expert mountain guide is the right fit. If your sales function relies on web hits, marketing campaigns, and lead-generation activities, sales is an "active" function, relying on proactive marketing campaigns to deliver measureable results. If this describes your planned in-country sales process, all functions must be in place for active success to occur.

Responsive mountain guides perform as needed, requested, or as directed by others. Roles such as fulfillment and support are the first responders leaping into action with a customer call. Maintenance, repair, and fix-what's-broken services are classic responsive roles. Fulfillment functions, such as delivery, installation, and training, respond to events or actions in an implementation process.

Identifying the role and action orientation that the mountain guide will play is vital to delivering value for your customer. Your focus on reaching the in-country customer will help you select the right mountain guide as a partner.

Ability to Influence

Influence is a mash-up of power and action that will give your company and product offerings the best advantage in-country. Select a mountain guide with an appropriate ability to influence people, process, or policies that will affect your in-country success. Consider three fundamental attributes of the guide's ability to influence: 1) Is an individual or a group of people better suited? 2) Does the individual or group have the power and ability to affect change? 3) Is the mountain guide or group appropriately positioned to take action?

1. Do you need a **person or group of people** exerting power or taking action to cause change?

   Example: Toshi's team has been influential in economic policies.

Choosing the right representative to assist your company in-country depends on a combination of things: the type of offering, the growth stage, and your action expectations. Depending on your business needs, the mountain guide could be an agent, a contractor, a family conglomerate, a contract manufacturer, a franchise agent, or something else entirely. We will explore the variety of options later in this section.

2. Consider the **power** needed to affect, change, or control something or someone and the ability needed to change the development of things such as conduct, thoughts, or decisions.

   Example: Juan has influence over planning within the Ministry of Education.

   Determine the type of power that will be most helpful to you when entering a country. Powers that an influential representative has and uses include the following: network, connections, expertise, knowledge, authority, position, location, opinion, motive, empathy, leadership, charisma, interpersonal skills, qualifications, etc. Look for these qualities when interviewing and choosing a representative to work with. See the section "Select the Best" below.

3. Can the person or organization take **action** to cause needed change?

   Example: Andrea can influence his decision.

   Identify the type of actions that you want an in-country representative to perform for you. The type of action required will be very specific to your business development needs and might include the following: making introductions, setting up meetings, getting appointments with government or industry, training/educating company personnel, informing, hosting, negotiating, advising, selling, closing, etc. Be specific about the action you expect from your mountain guide. This will enable you to set the right objectives for a successful working relationship, as discussed in "Establish Agreement."

Types of Mountain Guides

Depending on your business, one mountain guide may provide all the assistance you need, or you may require other trail guides, each with specialized complementary skills. Robert has used agents extensively and refers to them as ambassadors.

The type of mountain guide you select will depend on the primary need of your business at your phase of entry. Each type of mountain guide will have different skills to bring to the table. They will excel in some areas and won't be able to accomplish other things. The most common mountain guides fall into one of the following categories:

* agent
* consultant
* contract manufacturer
* contractor
* exporter
* family conglomerate
* franchise agent
* joint venture
* licensing agent

Agent

You have a business opportunity to bring in-country, either B2B or B2C. Your agent should have industry-specific knowledge to assist you in navigating trade requirements, approvals, and business partners in-country. The agent should have a good industry-specific network, including appropriate government connections. The agent will connect you with partners/

buyers and will know the competitive landscape. Typically an agent will offer you a degree of exclusivity, not representing other competitive or similar offerings. Other trail guides may be needed depending on the agent's skill set. If you are considering an exclusive relationship, establish parameters of time, geography, or performance because there are risks if expectations are not met.

Consultant

You are looking for some specialized assistance. A consultant may work with or for your agent or contractor. A consultant will provide specific skills, capabilities, and contacts that will complement the work of your primary mountain guide, such as sales, marketing, industry, or government. When other trail guides are needed, there are likely to be consultants. You may use one or more depending on specific skills needed. They are typically employed on a short-term or project basis.

Contract Manufacturer

You have a product to produce in-country. Contract manufacturers can handle local labor, country approvals, localization, and inventory. The contract manufacturer should have a good B2B network. He or she won't connect you with buyers and won't know the competitive landscape. Other trail guides will be needed to connect you with buyers, such as a local distributor, contractor, or sales and marketing agent.

Contractor

A contractor is the same as an agent. The difference is that a contractor will typically not ask for exclusivity. Other trail guides may be necessary depending on the contractor's skill set. Carefully assess other similar or competitive products that he or she represents and how he or she will determine market placement for each product set.

Exporter

You have a turnkey product to introduce, either B2B or B2C. Exporters have knowledge of country trade requirements, transportation, inventory, and logistics. They will help you with the morass of paperwork required. Exporters should have a good logistics and industry-specific retail network. An exporter will know the competitive landscape (to a degree) and may connect you with buyers, depending upon your industry. Other trail guides, such as a local marketing agent or contractor, will be needed.

Family Conglomerate

A family conglomerate is similar to an agent, above, but the scope and reach of the relationship will be far more extensive. Family conglomerates will also have a network that includes financing and back-office services. You will leverage their in-country knowledge, network, and political capital. But, they will represent multiple interests and they may also bring political "baggage" as well. They should have a good industry-specific network, including appropriate government connections. They will connect you with partners and buyers. They will be knowledgeable about the in-country competitive landscape. Other trail guides may be required, depending on the skill set of the family conglomerate, but they will have to be acceptable to the family. Expect the family conglomerate to recommend and approve other trail guides, as they will want to keep them within their circle of influence. Carefully examine political relationships; they can work for you and against you.

Franchise Agent

You have a brand and turnkey business to franchise in-country. Franchise agents handle franchise localization, in-country approvals, and legal requirements. They should have a good industry, regulatory, and government network. They will understand the competitive landscape and should connect you to prospective buyers. Other trail guides such as local marketing agent or contractor will be required, depending on skill set.

Joint Venture
You have a solution, product, service, or business opportunity to bring in-country. In a joint venture, you will share risk and reward with the local partner. You will leverage the partner's in-country knowledge and political capital. The partner will leverage your offering, your expertise, and your investment. Partners should have a good customer network, linking the JV (joint venture) to buyers and users. They will connect you with buyers and will know the competitive landscape. Other trail guides will typically be handled by the JV, but you will want to be intimately involved with the selection of a local CEO. There can be significant risk on the extremes. If the JV is wildly successful or if it does not yield desired results, assess your options carefully.

Licensing Agent
You have a process, technology, or product to license in-country. A licensing agent can handle country approvals and legal requirements. The licensing agent should have a good legal, regulatory, and government network. He or she will understand the competitive landscape but probably won't connect you to prospective buyers. Other trail guides will include a local sales agent or contractor.

Select the Best

You want the best in everything you do. You want the best mountain guide. The type of mountain guide and business relationship you select will be unique to your products, the country, your target customers, and the way you want to do business. Never lose sight of the fact that your mountain guide is a sales agent, representing your company and selling for you. Your mountain guide needs to help you find customers.

Find the best mountain guide to meet your business needs. "What Mountain to Climb," above, defines the role, action orientation, and influential capabilities. This will narrow the playing field so that you can begin interviewing candidates.

The top five selection criteria are

* industry experience,
* experience with *relevant* offerings,
* length of sales cycle,
* type of business style, and
* territory.

There are many factors that will affect your selection process. Here are some important considerations that should be included in your interview questions and selection criteria:

Industry experience

* Does the mountain guide have prior experience within your particular industry? Will he or she "get" what you do? Will the mountain guide understand the types of people he or she will have to work with?

* Who does the mountain guide know, and who knows him or her? **America is the only country that does business with strangers.** Europeans, Asians, Africans, and South Americans do business by introduction. A trusted player in-country and within the industry will extend trust to your company. Your offering may be chosen not based on pricing or technology but possibly because of *who* made the introduction.

* Does the mountain guide have cross-industry experience? We agree with Mona Pearl in *Grow Globally*[25] that representatives with cross-industry experience have flexibility, open-mindedness, and more universal skills necessary to introduce new products into new markets. They are more likely to embrace solutions from outside their comfort zone.

Experience with relevant offerings

* Does the mountain guide have experience representing similar offerings in-country?

* Does he or she understand the challenges and know how to navigate around them with demonstrated prior successes?

* The mountain guide, whether a company or an individual, should be financially sound and resourceful. You don't want to be the guide's first client because a novice *doesn't* know what he or she *doesn't* know. You don't want to be a mountain guide's largest client or smallest client.

* When your mountain guide is a company, you can obtain financial information from other sources, such as Dun & Bradstreet or region-specific sources. For a reasonable fee, these services will provide data on your representatives, partners, and customers, such as ownership, activity and financial status.

Length of the sales cycle

* With what length of sales cycle has the representative had the most success? People skilled at working with a short sales cycle look for rapid repeated feedback from the market to determine their course of action.

* People skilled in long sales cycles know how to build the customer-vendor relationship over time, continually building trust and adding value.

* A mismatch will result in a lack of sales traction and frustration for both you and your mountain guide.

Type of business style

* Business style should be humble yet confident. Arrogance is not respected in any market, either at home or abroad.

* Robert recommends hiring a mountain guide that is good at working with tangible products, not services. Even though you may be selling services, your goal is to package that service as a product. Service representatives are good at *customizing* an offering to meet customer needs. Product representatives are better at *positioning* an existing offering to meet the needs of the customer.

* What business approach has worked in the United States? What has worked in other countries? What does your prospective mountain guide expect will best suit in-country customers?

* If your offering requires a consultative approach, a mountain guide that is pushy will alienate customers and not be effective in a consultative sell.

Territory

* Can the mountain guide effectively cover the country or territory?

* What proximity is the mountain guide to the territory? Can he or she easily reach customer and government officials? Face-to-face contact is key.

* Will your mountain guide be able to build trust and respect in-country? If your offering improves factory automation, a representative based in Germany may be able to represent your company throughout Europe due to the global market's respect for German expertise in

factory automation. If your offering is high-end cosmetics, a French or Italian representative may be better able to represent your offering in-country.

Operational considerations need to be addressed. These questions are ones we like to ask in the interview process to learn more about the country and gain insight into how the mountain guide operates:

Market Considerations

* What is the best way to penetrate the target market?
* What type of add-on business or after-sales service would in-country customers expect?
* Is it advantageous to be an American supplier? Why or why not?

Marketing Costs

* What is the most productive way to reach in-country customers?
* Outline an example of a cost-effective marketing campaign.

Proposal Considerations

* Describe the typical proposal process.
* Will detailed proposals be required in the local language? If so, how would you suggest we handle that?

Technical Knowledge

* What level of technical depth is involved at various steps of the decision process?

* How do decision-makers view in-country technical expertise versus external expertise?

Last checkpoint in the selection: Do you and the mountain guide actually like each other? Chemistry is important. You will "live together" when you are in-country and talk two to three times a week when you are away. It's like dating. **If you don't like the person, the relationship won't work.** If you have a trusted, respected, and cohesive relationship, it will be apparent to you, your customers, and your partners. If you don't, it will be equally apparent.

Robert and Janet give prospective mountain guides "homework" between visits. This provides mountain guides an opportunity to demonstrate their skills, and you can see how effectively they communicate, how responsive they are, and what insights they will bring to your business.

"Homework" can provide you with invaluable market information to use in the launch in-country. Don't abuse the privilege by asking for too much before you have establish a working relationship.

Following are examples of some of our favorite pre-hire homework assignments. We rarely assign more than one before establishing a formal relationship or agreement.

* *Competition*: Who are the major competitors in-country? What is the sales and marketing strategy of the market leader? Why do customers prefer the market leader over other alternatives?

* *Government*: What ministries or departments regulate this industry in-country? What is the forecast and trend for regulatory oversight? What are the opinions of the mountain guide's connections within the controlling ministry telling them?

* *Buyers*: Who would the mountain guide see as the best candidates for initial proof-of-concept customers? What benefits, unique to his or

her country, are important to customers? Who would be involved in the review and decision?

Meet your prospective mountain guide in-country. Meet with him or her several times and in several locations—at your hotel, over dinner, and at his or her office.

Visiting the mountain guide's place of business will provide greater insight into the size of his or her operation, specialty, diversification, and overall way of doing business. If you are working with an organization, rather than a single individual, visiting the office also makes it easier to meet senior members of the organization and top managers. If the mountain guide is an individual, he or she will also have a location where business is conducted. Individual representatives overseas, like those in the United States, will have a location where they do business such as a rented office, coffee shop, borrowed office space, or the like. Bear in mind that appearances can be deceiving; a very humble operation may have very good contacts for your business.

Jik Chu has some additional insight into selecting and working with mountain guides.

More Stories over Tea and Skype with Jik Chu
Relationships can be tricky. Be on the lookout for subtle relationship risks. Jik Chu emphasizes the importance of hiring a mountain guide that you can trust and one that will be loyal to your company. It is not easy. Intricate in-country relationships require trust and loyalty.

Jik Chu is a mountain guide for South Korea. A South Korean native, he attended college in the United States and experienced working with both US and Korean companies. Jik shared two interesting trend alignment stories with us in chapter 2, "Add Value."

Story 1: Check behind the Scenes
American companies are not accustomed to the combination of business and politics that are more common in other countries. Behind-the-scenes

political activities can be brewing while a company is naïvely acting in good faith.

An American pharmaceutical company had been working with a large Korean pharma manufacturer. The American company had been selling chemical compounds to the Korean pharma and wanted to establish a joint venture (JV) to increase profit margins. Having worked with the Korean manufacturer for a few years, the American company's employees felt they understood and could trust the Korean company.

Unknown to the American pharmaceutical company, multiple Korean pharmas, including the American company's manufacturing partner, had been lobbying the government to ***not*** *grant JV licenses. Their interest was to keep business under the sole direction of Korean management.*

The American company pressed forward, hiring Jik as the JV's local CEO. Jik had strong contacts in the "blue house" (Korea's equivalent of the White House). He effectively lobbied government officials and obtained a JV license on a 50:50 equity ratio.

The CEO of the Korean pharma capitulated to the JV agreement but hated Jik for it and worked behind the scenes to have Jik removed. The JV ran successfully for fifteen years, but not all the decisions were favorable to the American company, as the Korean pharma controlled many choices. The JV shifted from 50:50 to 51:49 in favor of the Korean company. The American company was given no choice for sales other than using the Korean pharma's distribution network.

Jik Chu's lesson to learn: hire people and make partnerships with those that you can trust and who will be loyal to you. "If one person gets into trouble with the local partner, hire a new one." Don't proceed without someone you can trust.

Story 2: Investigate Dragging Feet

When things change in an otherwise good relationship, look a little deeper for the cause.

A large Canadian company was working with a Korean company as its sales partner. The Korean sales partner was selling the Canadian products with good margin. Sales were robust, and relationships were good between the two companies, with mutual respect and knowledge sharing.

The Canadian company came out with an exciting new next-gen product, expecting the Korean partner to embrace the new offering with enthusiasm. Instead, the opposite occurred. The Korean sales partner was dragging its feet and would not take on the new product. The Canadian company was perplexed; it projected more sales and higher margin for both companies.

The relationship struggled and faltered. The Canadian company failed to see that its Korean sales partner was developing its own competitive product. Eventually it dumped the Canadian products for its own.

Jik Chu's lesson: hire partners you trust, but when behavior changes, look more deeply for the cause. "When a local partner decides to drag their feet, there is little the company can do other than appoint another partner, contract permitting. But, expect this to cause disruption in the marketplace."

Story 3: Watch for Hidden Agents

High-flying, fast-moving markets are exhilarating and risky. Trends were turning into megatrends and affecting an industry with incredible change and technological development. Large established businesses, start-up companies, and government-backed utilities were contending, collaborating, competing, and cooperating. It was nearly impossible to pick the winner.

Jik was working with a company that was on one side of this wave of technology change. Jik lobbied intensely with government, industry, and public opinion. What Jik failed to see on the other side was a start-up with close relationships to a single very highly placed official that acted as a hidden agent. This highly placed official was able to affect key legislation for this trending industry change in Korea. The company that Jik represented was not able to proceed in Korea.

Jik Chu's lesson: "Look for hidden agents of the competition from the beginning."

Looking back on history now, Jik represented the technology and the company that ultimately dominated the industry worldwide. So much of Jik's energy, time, and angst was expended on the Korean market, which took a different path due to the hidden agent. His company's later market domination is nothing more than bitter consolation now.

Good Representatives Are Selective Too

As you interview prospective mountain guides, you should expect them to interview you as well. Tap into all those management and interview skills that you have used over the years. It is much the same. As with any interview, expect that a thoughtful candidate will ask you questions.

Look at the kind of questions your candidate mountain guide asks: strategic, insightful, operational, tactical, or none. (None? No, not really.)

The type of questions provides insight into how the mountain guide thinks and the level at which he or she will function. Strategic and insightful questions are good indicators of a mountain guide that will be more self-directed and plan a course of action. Candidates with more operational and tactical questions will likely require more management direction and guidance. Here are examples of types of questions a candidate might ask:

- Strategic
  - What impact will success in *this country* (fill in the blank) have on your company and its global plan?

* Why have you selected *this country* to enter at this time?
* Have you done business in *this country* before? With whom? What was the outcome?

- Insightful
  * Describe customer retention? Customer support?
  * What international trade associations, business associations, or other affiliations does your company have?
  * Tell me about your other international representatives. What's working? What isn't? Will representatives meet periodically to share best practices?

- Operational
  * Who will be available to help me after the training?
  * Do you have any bonus programs associated with achieving results, such as exceeding goals, recruiting other agents, etc.?

- Tactical
  * Do you provide training? How many days or hours of formal training? Is there a cost to me?
  * What type of marketing materials and website services are available?

As with any interview, you can get a glimpse into the underlying motivation of a prospective representative by the questions asked. A mountain guide will have a combination of personal, professional, social, and organizational drivers motivating him or her.

If questions center on compensation, income potential is important to your mountain guide. From an American perspective, money motivation can be viewed as a good thing. In other countries, it may be a **speed bump** signaling trouble with individual or business income. Individuals who are purely money motivated may make bad decisions as they represent your company because their goal is to maximize their own personal income.

If questions focus on job creation or economic development, it means the mountain guide may be focused on working for the good of the country. This can be an important motivator as your representative will envision his or her role in a cause greater than self. It can also signal a **speed bump** if strong nationalistic bias might hinder your company's success in-country; you'll have to decide.

If questions emphasize goals and outcome, achievement may be the mountain guide's priority. This can be an **accelerator** as representatives motivated by personal and professional achievement tend to be the most successful. It is also an approach that Americans are very comfortable with, so it's likely to work well with your management style.

Feeling pressed? You have a sense of urgency. Time is of the essence. Your boss is asking about making progress. Alert: **barrier** ahead. Take a deep breath. Don't make the mistake of selecting the first representative that you interview. If you do, your decision will likely disappoint you later.

Selecting the mountain guide takes time; don't rush it. Give the selection process the courtesy of your careful consideration. Initial interviews can be conducted via Skype, phone, or WebEx, but **you *must* travel and meet with candidates, face-to-face** in-country. This provides more breadth and depth for an informed decision by allowing you to dive more deeply into the pool of information of how the mountain guide presents himself or herself.

Establish Agreement

There are two critical layers to the business arrangement: legal agreement and working agreement.

The working agreement is the most critical because it provides the basis for both the legal arrangements and for your day-to-day activities. The focus here is on elements of the working agreement.

Contracts in some countries are not as important as the agreement made in person and agreed to with a bow or handshake. No matter what the in-country customs, you must write it down.

Look to legal counsel for assistance with the contractual agreement. It's not difficult or scary; there are standard agreements that can be modified to meet your particular business situation and in-country requirements. The type of mountain guide will determine the type of agreement. Whether you need a nondisclosure, registered agent, independent contractor, operating agreement, or something else entirely, your legal counsel can easily provide you with the right agreement.

The working agreement or operational guide can be presented as an MOU (memorandum of understanding) or other nonbinding agreement and should be signed by both parties. The working agreement outlines expectations, goals, and working arrangements. Robert prefers a simple table format, not more than two or three pages, written in plain English without a lot of legalese.

Working agreements should be reviewed, revised, and updated periodically. They will typically coincide with your company's fiscal cycles, but not necessarily. A working agreement will normally include the following eight main sections:

* parties
* engagement
* designated territory

* goals and objectives
* business development services
* compensation
* term and termination
* signature block

Parties are the participants entering into this agreement. They include

* the representative (mountain guide's name or business name) and
* your company and the person the mountain guide will report to

Engagement covers the type of engagement and purpose of working together.

* The type of engagement can be exclusive or nonexclusive, as defined herein. The mountain guide may be classified as agent, contractor, consultant, or other. (For ideas, review "Types of Mountain Guides.")
* Purpose of the engagement may be sales, expertise, fulfillment, or support. (For ideas, review "What Mountain to Climb?")

Designated Territory includes the focus of activities defined by relevant measures: geography, products and/or services, customers, or other determining factors. Details should include the following:

* specific geographic responsibility—country, region or city
* your specific company products and/or services that the mountain guide will represent
* target customers the mountain guide is expected to contact—as appropriate to your business by vertical market, industry, or named-account or by horizontal market, functional responsibility, or job title
* a simple statement for flexibility (optional), such as this: "Designated territory to be discussed, reviewed, and agreed in writing by both parties in advance of any sales activity by (representative) on (company) behalf."

Goals and Objectives include a statement of measureable purpose specific to the nature of the relationship, such as revenue, customer capture, meetings, or other.

* If it's a monetary goal, it is typically expressed in USD, as a cumulative amount to be achieved within the time period of the working agreement.
* There should be a definition of revenue type—booking, revenue, or payment received. (For ideas, review commission in appendix 4, "Compensate and Motivate.")

Business Development Services should cover expectations of the role and type of services to be provided by the mountain guide, including milestones and reporting requirements.

* Role and services will be specific to the skills of the mountain guide and your stage of country entry and may cover the following:
  * hosting company employees, partners or customers
  * making government contacts
  * working with other in-country agents, as applicable
  * responding to inquiries
  * providing information on market conditions or trends
  * participating in trade shows or exhibits, as appropriate
* Milestones include calendar, fiscal, or project-related events with associated time frame, including actions associated with the milestones.
* Reporting encompasses issues such as in what form and on what time interval rolling sales are forecast, account information, and use of company CRM (customer resource management) or a separate reporting tool.
* This section will include specific statements, along with general guidelines such as: "(Representative) will at all times abide by and act in accordance with (Company) business policies."

Compensation includes outline of compensation, payment, and reimbursement. A separate agreement may be required to align with company policy.

* Compensation outline of applicable elements includes
  * retainer,
  * bonuses, and
  * other incentives.
* Responsibilities of the representative to present compensation request or expense reimbursement request, as applicable, should be stated.
* Expected payment time frame by the company should be included.
* For more ideas, see appendix 4, "Compensate and Motivate."

Term and Termination sets out the time frame of the agreement and how it can be concluded.

* This should include length of engagement as outlined in this agreement; a statement something like this: "Engagement will commence on an agreed effective date and terminate <u>(some number of)</u> months thereafter."
* Information on termination without cause should also appear; a statement something like this: "The Agreement may be terminated by either party for convenience at any time with thirty days prior written notice."
* Information on survivable terms of the agreement after termination should be stipulated, as well as how long the terms shall remain in force. For example, this could apply to commission (variable compensation) for some period of time following termination of the agreement.

Signature Block provides an indication of agreement and should include

* your signature or signature of other authorized company representative,
* the representative's (mountain guide's) or authorized party's signature, and
* date signed.

The working agreement pulls everything together: the type of mountain guide, expected role, the need he or she fulfills, why the person was selected, and compensation for him or her. The working agreement should be empowering and enabling, not restrictive and controlling. You are defining the rules of engagement and how you will work together to achieve results and success in-country.

Compensate and Motivate

A successful operation requires investment. Building your successful US business required investment in many resources: people, materials, energy, services, knowledge, office space, and more. Taking your business to another country will also require investment. **Invest in your mountain guide: use a compensation plan that excites and motivates while being budget friendly.**

If you want to **accelerate** your business, offer incentive plans that reward performance and loyalty, now and for the long term. Some companies require a cap on variable incentives; Robert thinks that is insane. A cap on incentives will throttle in-country efforts when they have an opportunity to accelerate faster.

Compensation structure should be part of a time-bounded agreement; this allows for revision at the end of the specified time frame. After initial market establishment, the time frame should be between two times (2X) and four times (4X) your known sales or turnover cycle. A company with an average three-month cycle would typically construct compensation plans that are six months or annual. Most compensation plans track to corporate fiscal cycles as well.

The key components are commission, retainer, bonuses, expense reimbursement, and other incentives.

* **Commission** is a variable compensation-plan element based on the achievement of specific financial goals, such as bookings, revenue, or payment received. Set expectations that commission and degree of difficulty go hand in hand. In the early stages of the mountain

guide relationship, commission will be high in recognition of the high degree of difficulty. In later stages of market development, as volume increases, commission may be less, commensurate with relative ease of doing business.

A story over Coffee with Kimberly Benson
Kimberly Benson, president of Zenaida Global, likes working on straight commission. It puts the responsibility on her shoulders to thoroughly examine the success potential of the company in the selected international markets. She is a proactive mountain guide. On straight commission she shoulders 100 percent of the risk and gives her clients high confidence in her ability to succeed. Kim also benefits from the success of an international venture—as sales increase, so do her commissions!

* **Retainer** is fixed compensation paid in advance for specified work. We use the term "retainer" for convenience, but your company may refer to fixed compensation with some other terminology, like "guarantee," "allowance," "budget," or something else. A retainer signifies that your company is entering a mutual action-oriented agreement with the mountain guide. It is best to structure retainer payment as building blocks based on specific work outlined in the working agreement.

Another Jik Chu Story over Tea and Skype
Jik Chu prefers to work on a compensation plan that combines retainer with variable compensation, such as commission or bonuses. This is because there is a great deal of work that is required for a company to enter a new country, such as government introductions, lobbying for new industry policies, and networking. Many of these critical activities don't directly result in sales. Jik works as an active and responsive partner assisting his client with whatever is necessary to ensure company success. He knows that to launch a company and product into a new market takes a great deal of time, preparation, and effort before profitable results can be achieved.

* **A bonus** is often added to a retainer as a reward for good performance or achieving specific goals, such as setting up meetings, finding qualified leads, signed MOUs, or obtaining proof-of-concept customers.

* **Expense reimbursement** is repayment for agreed-upon and actual out-of-pocket expenses incurred while performing the job. Expenses submitted for reimbursement should follow the same or similar process as used by employees in the United States, which will likely require receipts and justification (statement of purpose).

* **Other incentives** can excite and inspire action or greater effort; other incentives can be offered as a reward for increased productivity or high performance. Other incentives could include gifts, training, conferences, recognition, or other awards.

Explore appendix 4, "Compensate and Motivate," for more detail.

How to Find a Mountain Guide

There are a number of ways to find a mountain guide. The most common methods are to leverage your own network, employ an expat (expatriate) living in-country, or use government resources.

Start with your own network. Leverage your network for people that you know or referrals to an individual or organization that has served a similar purpose. The extended trust of reaching someone you are connected with helps to initiate conversations more quickly. In one company where Janet was looking to enter Europe, the initial country of entry was Spain because the company employed a Spanish national who was interested and willing to help. He initiated connections to a great mountain guide, which made entry into Spain seamless. Later, this Spanish national offered to move back "home," which accelerated company growth even faster, as he knew the company, product, and business very well. From a solid starting point in Spain, he quickly built connections into other countries with appropriate distributors to handle sales, inventory, and services.

Retired executives with relevant industry or government experience can be a great resource. Robert has used this approach successfully on multiple occasions. Robert leverages his network as well as government resources to identify people in-country that fit the needed mountain guide profile. Retired executives will have a deep and wide network that they trust and that trusts them. They enjoy the role of mountain guide because it keeps them connected. They also bring the value of significant years of in-country experience. Jik Chu is a retired executive and wonderful mountain guide; his stories are worth their weight in gold for valuable lessons, things to avoid, perspective, and humor.

Expats can also make interesting mountain guides. An expat is an individual who typically was relocated by an employer to a country to help establish the company's business in a region or specific country. Expats know how US companies operate, speak excellent English, and will make you feel comfortable that they will make entering the country an easy transition. If they have been with a competitor in-country or related business, they will understand some of the issues you will face when importing your offering. It's good to understand their reasons for continuing to reside in-country rather than returning to the United States. Their knowledge of the US industry could be stale, especially if they have been outside the United States for more than five years. Their network of contacts will not be as wide or deep as a retired executive's but will still be relevant and valuable.

Another effective method is to use US government resources. There are export events conducted in the United States and in-country with the goal of promoting US exports and connecting US companies with potential representatives and buyers. Contact the US Embassy both in the United States and in-country. Do your research. Search for resources using federal, state, and local government websites to find events or more customized single-company activities. Export.gov is a useful federal resource. Many states and larger US cities also have consulates for specific countries that promote trade and will help to connect you with potential representatives. Check appendix 1, "Resources and References," for suggestions of where to begin your research.

People accomplish amazing things, from great architects, athletes, and scientists to musicians, authors, and businesspeople. You can think of an endless list of amazing individuals: Frank Lloyd Wright, Babe Ruth, Albert Einstein, Mick Jagger, John Steinbeck, and countless others. What you don't think of necessarily are the many other individuals who combine their talents with the talents of others to achieve great things as a team. The team may be on the field or behind the scenes, but every great achievement requires a team.

Companies, like people, are able to accomplish amazing things by combining their efforts with the skills and influence of others. When Apple first launched the iPhone in 2007, it partnered with AT&T Mobile for distribution. This helped Apple seize eighteen in eighteen: an unprecedented 18 percent market share just eighteen months after launch.[26] McDonald's world-famous Happy Meal is consistently co-branded with the latest kid-popular TV and movie characters. It is the co-branding of two famous icons, the Happy Meal and SpongeBob or Batman, which captures the attention of kids and adults alike.

A mountain guide is your in-country representative. Your mountain guide could be a single star individual, like Michael Jordan or John Elway, or it could be an organization or team. Your mountain guide should be influential in-country, within your industry sector, and with prospective customers.

The right representative will deliver the desired results. Where would a great author like John Steinbeck be without a publisher, or Frank Lloyd Wright's architectural designs without a builder? Working on a team adds skills, talent, and ideas—like the Rolling Stones added to Mick Jagger's stardom or the New York Yankees contributed to Babe Ruth's fame and success. Where will you be if you don't have the right mountain guide or team behind you? The right mountain guide is a vital part of your team. He or she adds necessary knowledge and complementary skills and helps reduce unnecessary risk to deliver the best possible results for your business.

Assess Your Ability to Climb the Mountain

① Selection of Your Mountain Guide

1. Define the **role** the mountain guide will fulfill for your company: sales, expertise, fulfillment, support, or something else? What mountain do you want your mountain guide to climb? Write it down (hmmm, you've heard that suggestion before).

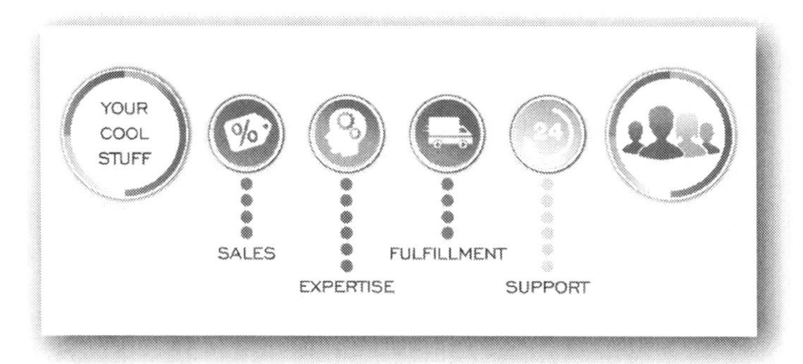

2. What role or **action orientation** is most critical: proactive, active, or responsive?

   - ☐ Proactive action orientation best aligns to the sales role. Depending upon industry norms, this may also be desired in fulfillment or support.
   - ☐ Active action orientation best aligns to expertise-driven roles. But, depending on your lead generation model, it could be applicable to sales.
   - ☐ Responsive action orientation best aligns to fulfillment and support roles.

3. What **type** of mountain guide best fills your need: agent, consultant, contract manufacturer, contractor, exporter, family conglomerate, franchise agent, joint venture, licensing agent, or something else? Spend some additional time reviewing the table "Types of Mountain Guides."

② Structure for Your Mountain Guide

1. Do you have a mountain guide?

   ☐ NO ☐ YES

   * If no, skip the rest of the assessment questions in this chapter, and go find one!

2. Is a written working agreement in place?

   ☐ NO ☐ YES

   * If no, put one together.

3. Do you have a compensation structure in place?

   ☐ NO ☐ YES

   * If no, time to construct a plan to compensate and motivate your mountain guide.

③ Strength of Your Mountain Guide

1. Does your mountain guide currently reside within the designated territory?

   ☐ NO ☐ YES

   * If no, why? What are travel considerations? Will this affect reimbursable expenses? Are there any other considerations?

2. Is your mountain guide a native speaker, fluent in the language of the country, or conversational?

   ☐ Native ☐ Fluent ☐ Conversational

   * If not a native speaker, how will this be perceived in-country?

3. Is the majority of the mountain guide's relevant work experience in country?

   ☐ NO ☐ YES

   * If no, how do you think this will affect their ability to perform the role you have agreed to?

4. What is the level of relevant and related industry experience?

   ☐ None ☐ Minimal ☐ Some ☐ Strong ☐ Extensive

   * If none or minimal, how do you think this will affect the person's ability to perform the role you have agreed to?

5. Does the role of your mountain guide include sales?

   ☐ NO ☐ YES

   * If yes, what is his or her relevant sales experience in vertical market you are targeting and with the decision-makers (management-level and functional responsibility)?
   * If yes, has he or she worked with sales cycles of the same length?
   * If yes, has he or she worked with a similar sales process?

5. Based on the interview questions the mountain guide asked you, how do you perceive his or her working style? Rank your perception on a 1 to 4 scale, with 1 as the strongest attribute and 4 as the weakest.

   * Tactical ____________
   * Strategic ____________
   * Operational ____________
   * Insightful ____________

Chapter 5

Build Trust

The conversation was strange and uncomfortable. Maurice kept talking about dating—relationships, parents, and family. Alex had met Maurice at a small quiet coffee shop to talk business, or so he thought.

Maurice quoted some marriage expert, Hellen Chen, who said that 85 percent of relationships inevitably end in a breakup; that meant that only an elite few ended in marriage. Even more surprising, Maurice told Alex that 85 percent of US manufacturers don't export their product; only a meager 15 percent do. Wow! Alex was shocked.

It was even more unexpected to find that this export ratio has been much the same for the last three to four decades! How could this be, when the United States consistently ranks among the top five world exporters?[27]

Alex asked the obvious question, "Why ***don't*** *85 percent of US manufacturers export their products?"*

Maurice calmly responded, "For the same reasons that so many relationships fail."

"Within the couple's relationship, there are lots of trust issues, different expectations, different interests, and different priorities," continued Maurice. "Not to mention interference from parents and family. The coupling of the in-country customers and a company's offering also has a lot of complexity. It needs to be a relationship of mutual value and trust."

Yes, that made sense, thought Alex.

"Internal resistance from the parent company and its family of partners is the number-one barrier to taking companies international," Maurice explained.

Alex considered this to be quite strange. He sipped his coffee slowly, savoring the flavors as he contemplated this further. Why would companies get in their own way, creating their own barriers, when international growth offered such great potential?

Hmmm. Maybe TolpaTek wasn't much different. Alex could see the resistance; yes, there were risks, costs, and complicated paperwork to deal with. But following the ***Built for Global*** *de-risk formula had helped Alex address many of the company's fears. Cynthia, the CFO, worried about not getting paid. Martin in manufacturing was afraid of complicated shipping paperwork, which ultimately could be handled by TolpaTek's freight-forwarding partner.*

Alex had witnessed more subtle, subjective, and invasive concerns, like unrealistic internal expectations and unwillingness to involve or trust partners. There were times when it seemed that Alex and his company were moving through life at different speeds.

He had to laugh. Maurice was right after all. International business is a lot like dating! All the same issues of compatibility, communication, and trust.

Relationships cannot last without trust. Trust is the foundation of every strong relationship, personal and professional. Trust is operating with integrity and transparency and being open and honest yet holding in confidence those matters meant to remain private.

Trust forms the foundation of success. Trust and success for your home team, in the new market, and with your customers. Without the strength of trust in all three of these relationships, you cannot succeed over time.

Figure 18: Trust is the foundation of relationships

Trust is the Bubble Wrap of business. It wraps around every precious business relationship, cushioning the relationship from impact.

When business is running smoothly, the cushion of Bubble Wrap becomes greater, providing more protection. Those little bubbles of trust are filled with more trust, creating bigger bubbles of trust that guard the relationship in turbulent times. When things get bumpy, the trust that has been built keeps the business relationship intact and safeguards it from breaking.

When trust is broken, popping those delicate bubbles, look out!

POW! No transparency.
POP! Poor performance.
SNAP! Dishonesty.
WHAM! Fraud.
BANG!

If you are lucky, you can rebuild trust. But you will need to do things significantly different, and it will take time. POP! BAM! Worst case, it's impossible to rebuild the trust. Pack up and return home.

The Bubble Wrap of trust is strong and powerful. It is also very delicate and fragile. Bubble Wrap is nothing more than plastic wrap and air, yet we put it into service protecting the most priceless items through gorilla shipping.

Built for Global. Build for new markets. Build for trust.

Build Trust with the Home Team

A Story over Coffee with Kimberly Benson

There is no Easy Button for international success. Kimberly Benson, president of Zenaida Global, emphasizes that there are multiple factors required for successful international advancement.

Building trust within your own company is one essential factor that cannot be overlooked, she says. The trust built with your home team will help build the right international plan, assess risks, and solve problems.

Kim illustrated the need for trust by recounting a time when she was working with a high-end kitchen appliance manufacturer. The manufacturer's target market was the luxury buyer, not the mass market. The company hired Kim as their international department; she was its mountain guide for exporting.

Early in the relationship, Kim traveled to the company's Mississippi headquarters and met with key people in every department. She listened and learned about the mission, vision, and strategies. With each conversation Kim asked about their concerns and considerations for international operations. Several departments took some convincing because they would have to do things differently. This valuable communication led to collaboration, clarity, and consensus.

Marketing wanted to maintain a consistent message throughout the entire global marketplace, but Kim knew that distributors should be the face of the company in-country because appealing to the luxury buyer needed to be fine-tuned for each market. She told marketing that global, one-message advertising is typically not effective. The trust Kim built with marketing helped staff to see the need to offer distributors flexibility to use the US ads or to create their own. This flexibility became crucial to distributors in Brazil during a US economic downturn. The company had shifted to more folksy and homey positioning, which turned-off luxury buyers in Brazil. Brazil's wealthy buyers were attracted to exclusive sophistication, not down-home, unpretentious style.

Finance was comfortable with the straightforward pricing methodology used with distributors across the United States. It was difficult for finance to swallow that costs and prices would vary from country to country. Import duties could add 20 to 30 percent or more to the cost-basis. Countries with a US FTA (free-trade agreement) in place, could avoid these added import duties, like Mexico and Canada under NAFTA (North American FTA). Kim was crucial in helping this high-end appliance manufacturer realize that the variation in duty rates was important. Duty rates can make a difference between a viable distribution structure in a market and failure to penetrate a market because pricing is out of alignment with buyers. Kim helped the company make smart decisions on which countries to enter.

Technical support had to assist distributors and customers around the globe with varied wiring, power requirements, time zones, and more. Introducing one country at a time, with its unique variations, allowed for technical services to evolve in step with the international expansion.

Kim takes an inclusive approach to attracting new distribution partners. When interviewing a prospective distribution partner, she engages peers in both companies to get acquainted. Kim has learned that distributors "will often promise the world," but the key to turning these promises into reality is to encourage peer-to-peer conversations, from technology to marketing. This communication puts the promises and realities of both parties into alignment.

Another more subtle area often needing alignment is the difference in management styles. These differences can spark conflict in everything from distribution to logistics to branding. Kim prides herself on facilitating understanding between the dynamics of owners, managers, and staff within each of these entities to create successful, sustainable export relationships.

At home in the factory, whenever Kim sets up a new distributor and sold appliances into a new country, she would order the nation's flag. The flag would be hung over the production floor in Mississippi. It was a colorful and profound reminder to workers and visitors that this Mississippi production line touched the lives of people around the globe.

To successfully take a company into international markets, you must build upon personal relationships. Kim Benson of Zenaida Global is an expert at forging healthy, mutually beneficial business relationships. She starts by building strong support with the home team and extends that trust into each market she enters. In the five years that Kim worked with this appliance manufacturer, the flags grew in number from ten to forty, and then eighty.

You want to take your company into a new country. Don't go it alone. It's important to have support from the home team. Enlist support and positive influencers; even neutral players will help you and become more positive as momentum builds. You cannot successfully take a company international without a home team. **Look to build cross functional, organization support.** That may not sound easy, but as you can see from Kim's example, it is not that difficult either.

The whole company does not need to be behind the international effort, but a few well-positioned supporters appropriate to the stage of international development are essential.

The home team does not need to report to you or be in your organizational chain of command. In fact, it's often more valuable if your home team is *outside* of your direct organizational control. Sounds crazy, but by being independent of your organization, it adds to the perception of the team's impartiality and objective point of view.

The home team is your representative when you are not around. These people represent international operations in staff meetings. And even more importantly, in the more relaxed and informal conversations around the coffee pot, they provide support.

Building a Home Team: The Four Cs

Communication, consensus, collaboration, and clarity give strength to trusting relationships with colleagues, managers, and other departments. The four Cs fill the bubbles of trust for your home team. We live in a gorilla world of pressure, priorities, deadlines, competition, and more. The four Cs will help safely build the relationships to navigate international business and enter new markets.

The four Cs **accelerate** your ability to attract members, strengthen the commitment, and expand the influence of the home team.

1. **Communication.**
   Consistently communicate a clear vision, mission, and goal. Reinforce your strategy and objectives regularly. Show progress with small advancements and small wins on a continuous basis. Set expectations and be realistic, yet optimistic. Set the right goals: goals you can achieve.

2. **Consensus.**
   Build consensus that international growth for your company is a good thing. Convey how individual effort can make a difference and accomplish a lot. Help each member of your home team understand his or her role and impact; everyone likes to make a difference.

3. **Collaboration.**
   "All of us are smarter than any one of us."[28] The best way to get the job done right is to collaborate with others. You have more brains working on the challenge. Repeatedly thank and praise those who participate, both privately and publically.

4. **Clarity.**
   Well-defined roles for individuals and departments promote participation and eliminate confusion. Establish your international strategy. Be clear that roles, goals, and strategies will be refined over time as your company's global smarts advance.

Consistent exercise of the four Cs will build a strong home team. Without a home team, individuals and departments will become "international business prevention" agents. You don't want *that* to happen.

Who should be on the home team?

The size and character of the home team will vary depending on company maturity and level of international operations. Who's in and who's out changes with business need.

In all cases a representative from finance must be on the home team. You will be dealing with new currency, tariffs, and order processing as you gain momentum.

Human resources will not be on the home team until after you have gotten traction and if/when you decided to hire a full-time employee in-country.

Public companies should always include investor and media relations on the home team.

If this is your company's **first foray** outside the United States, the home team needs to include

* engineering
* product management, and
* finance.

The primary focus is on hitting milestones and objectives. Whether your company is a large-public enterprise, a successful midsize operation, or an early-stage business, you will need supportive assistance for technical compliance, product adaptation, and handling new currency. Add investor relations to the home team if your company is publically traded because business changes can affect investor perspective.

Companies that have already experienced **some success** outside of the United States have an experienced baseline, and the home team should include the management team.

The goal is to assess what has worked and what hasn't in current international operations so that the right decisions can be made regarding a new country or region to enter. Irrespective of the size of the company, if you are already dabbling with success outside the United States, you need to consider the options:

1) Do you invest in a new market *and* continue investing in existing markets? There is the risk of spreading resources too thin.

2) Do you invest in a new market *and* pull out of an existing market? This would focus more resources on the new market. There are also consequences that must be considered in the existing market—residual customer support, reputation impact, and global brand.

3) Do you *not* invest in a new market *and* add to the investment in the current market? If the existing market is realizing some success, maybe success can be accelerated with additional commitment and investment.

	INTERNATIONAL EXPERIENCE		
	FIRST FORAY	SOME SUCCESS	STRONG SUCCESS
HOME TEAM	EMPHASIS		
PRODUCT MGMT./ ENGR	★★★★★	★★	★
FINANCE / LEGAL	★★★★	★★★	★★
MARKETING	★★★	★★★★	★★★
SALES	★★	★★★★	★★★★
CUSTOMER SUPPORT	★	★★	★★★★★

Figure 19: Home team varies with experience

Companies with **strong regional** international success have already figured out a winning formula. The overarching objective is the velocity and extent of expansion. Do you want to continue expansion or "go for it," expanding into new regions for more expansive international expansion? A clear, consistent message about global strategy is important both internally and externally. Extending the winning formula into a new international region will require cross functional support from internationally active departments:

* marketing
* sales
* customer support

Should the CEO be on the home team? In an early-stage or start-up company, the answer is *yes*, without hesitation. Smaller and young companies have limited resources, and it's important that they are used mindfully. Successful midsized companies have a different set of decisions, and the CEO (chief executive officer) may or may not be on the home team depending upon company size. Expanding international operations for a midsized business should be strategically aligned with company growth goals. In large public companies, the home team will include divisional leadership but typically not the CEO. Larger public companies have divisional autonomy with divisional P&L (profit and loss), thus operating much like their own standalone business.

Should "outsiders" be on the home team? Enlist some unlikely team members: look for passion. International business often gets started at a trade show or with a call to the company. The person making this first connection sees the potential. That's the reason he or she passed it along to you in the first place. Even if this person doesn't fit the perfect home team profile, keep him or her connected and enthusiastic about your international efforts. The original contact was made by this not-so-perfect home team member because he or she is in a customer-facing role. They just may bring you new ideas and other international contacts that may help your cause.

What's in it for the Home Team?

People will want to be on your home team for all sorts of reasons. Look to understand *his or her* reasons and motivations. Reasons and motivations can be a complex mix of individual, social, or organizational.[29] That complex mix can be driven to action by an equally complicated blend of wants and needs. If you can tap into the power of *his or her* reasons and motivations, you will have committed team members. Home-team members thrive on communication in the four Cs.

"This sounds like fun!" is the sign of someone who is individually motivated. Everyone likes doing something enjoyable. When a person derives personal satisfaction from doing something, he or she will put in extra effort and go the extra mile. He or she may even hope to get an international business trip out of it. After all, a trip to Cairo sounds a lot more exciting than a trip to Cleveland. The flip side is that people avoid things they don't enjoy, eventually dropping out.

Watch out *for pleasure seekers who just think this looks like fun but have no real intent to contribute.*

"I can help with that!" is another indication of individual motivation. This is someone who wants to participate because of his or her ability to share or acquire knowledge, skills, or abilities. This is someone capable, able to perform well in a given situation, and performance motivated. Internal drive can come from the ability to use language skills and revitalize past proficiencies or add new ones. As performance-motivated people participate, they may drop out if things get too challenging, if they don't think they can do the job, or if they don't understand their roles. To get back to the four Cs, these home-team members thrive on consensus and collaboration. Embrace those who want to help solve problems and satisfy customer need.

Watch out *for big egos and arrogance—people who haven't appropriately assessed their skills.*

"This looks good!" is something a socially or organizationally motivated person might say. There could be any number of reasons that someone is socially or organizationally motivated—from recognition, to peer pressure, to social norms. For these people, the benefit could be building their résumés or curriculum vitae, being recognized among their peers, standing out, or possibly being promoted. If they think this "will look bad" or don't see the relative

value as compared to others, they may run screaming in the other direction. If they don't think they will be recognized for their contribution, they may also choose not to play. In the four Cs, consensus is important to them.

Watch out *for the greedy and the egotists who are looking for a free ride to being important.*

"*I love being on a great team!*" is another sign of a socially or organizationally motivated person. People like to work with people they trust, respect, and enjoy being with. People like working on a cause that has greater impact and is "bigger than yourself." With teamwork as the main motivator, they see reputation, recognition, and contribution as additional benefits. The unique status of being a pioneer for international markets and a member of your elite team will be a driver for them. If they don't think it's a team or that there will be inadequate organizational support for the cause, they may not apply full effort, or they may participate at first but then drop out. Of the four Cs, collaboration is critical for these home-team players.

Watch out *for people that are tired of what they are doing and looking to catch a free ride on the next big wave.*

For each home-team member, there is a complex combination of "big reasons why" they want to participate. For some it is the desire to actively contribute to company's growth, expansion, and acceleration—find those people and get them on the team. For others, the "big why" driving them is the satisfaction that accompanies the acceptance of your products and services globally—find them and recruit them to join the team. There is more support to be found at home than you might initially believe!

Beware of *Monsieur Saboteur*

Influence can be positive, working in your favor and accelerating your efforts to move into international markets. Or internal influence can just as easily be negative, working against you, slowing down progress, or stopping it all together. Influence[30] comes in all sizes shapes and shapes, it can appear at all levels of the organization, and it is neither male nor female.

Positive influencers are recommenders and helpers; they watch your back, provide assistance, and get things done. Positive influencers offer important information, uncover opportunities, and help avoid obstacles. They want you to be successful. Good business is reciprocal and your success is their success, either directly or indirectly.

Negative influencers can start as neutral or nonsupporters but later become naysayers, gatekeepers, vetoers, and even enemies to your international efforts. This type of person is *Monsieur Saboteur*. He is not someone you want joining your team when you have been working long hours to expand your company into new international markets. Yes, despite the name, *Monsieur Saboteur* is not French or French-speaking, as our catchy name might suggest, and he is just as often a she.

Influence	Characteristics
Positive Influencer	+ Works with you. Willing to invest time and effort + Thinks this is important (to them individually, the company, or the industry) + Provides information and assistance + Wants to make this work
Neutral Player	o Willing to invest some time to learn about what you are doing o Undecided, shows no preference or is ambivalent o Can't see the value o Could seem agreeable that it "might" work
Monsieur Saboteur Negative Influencer	– Will not work with you or share information – Believes that this change may be detrimental (to them individually, or to the company) – Will work against you or at best just do nothing – May or may not be open about his or her position

Figure 20: Positive, neutral, and negative influence

Amazing people and great companies need to surround themselves with supportive and positive influences to achieve great things. As we said before, architects need builders, contractors, and building owners. Athletes need coaches, competitors, and a team. Scientists need laboratories, scientific journals, collaborative colleagues, and the scientific community. Musicians need music media, backup instruments, and listeners. Authors need editors, publishers, and readers. Each benefits from communication, consensus, and collaboration, influencing one another to achieve great things.

Surround yourself with positive influencers. It's totally rewarding and fun.

Don't wear optimistic blinders. Be prepared. *Monsieur Saboteur* awaits your international arrival. Guaranteed—he (or she) is not who you might first think of. *Monsieur Saboteur* walks the halls of your company; he (or she) will not be readily obvious and will not be at the top of the organizational hierarchy.

The greatest **barrier**, interference, or incapacitation to going global comes from inside your own organization. Some "interference" is well meaning, while other is downright premeditated destruction. Beware. Stay on guard for *Monsieur Saboteur.*

Monsieur Saboteur will be calling. Guaranteed.

Monsieur Saboteur can take many different forms.

Unrealistic expectations from Mr. Expectations is one form of sabotage. Unrealistic expectations can kill international sales efforts before they have an opportunity to show progress. An important part of your success will depend on setting realistic goals and expectations for progress. Developing sales in a new country will take longer than anyone expects. Ramping up sales volume will also take longer than expected. Set reasonable expectations. In the four Cs, focus on communication: "under promise and over deliver."[31]

Lack of clarity from Ms. Fuzzy can be another type of sabotage. Lack of a clearly defined and communicated international strategy can lead to Ms. Fuzzy blocking your path in any number of departments from engineering to order processing. Communicate your strategy, objectives, and plans. It does not need to be in great detail, but let Ms. Fuzzy know that international expansion is a promise of the future. With clarity, she will work with you, not against you.

Management prekill of your international expansion can happen. "We've always been successful doing it this way; why change?" from Ms. Conventional is another form of sabotage. Poor communication and poor management process may encourage her to entrench her resistance to the global opportunities you advocate. Spend time understanding the perceived risks, from her point of view. There may be some important components you have missed and can address. More likely, there are important risk-reduction steps you have taken that Ms. Conventional is not aware of. As appropriate, build consensus by involving her in select meetings, collaborate on certain decisions, and get her buy-in.

Reluctance from Mr. Suspicious to involve or trust external partners, like your mountain guide, can slow or stop international process. This lack of trust typically comes from one of two areas: Mr. Suspicious may not believe that your international partners are competent enough to get the job done, or he may believe that their intentions are not honorable. You can help Mr. Suspicious support your international efforts by offering proof of the mountain guide's ability in past successful endeavors. Consider collaborating with Mr. Suspicious on the skills requirements and work objectives for the mountain guide. Gain agreement on the goals, communicate actions, and share results to help diffuse his concerns.

Do your best to understand why each individual described above is in this negative position. Men and women are equally likely to represent any of these negative perspectives. Understanding what influences their position will help you to minimize, neutralize, or eliminate the impact. Reread the section "What's in It for the Home Team" to come up with ideas. The four Cs (communication, consensus, collaboration, and clarity) provide straightforward approaches to reducing the impact of Monsieur Saboteur or eliminating his or her presence all together.

Be realistic. We are; that's what *Built for Global* is all about. There will be times when it will be frustrating, challenging, and discouraging. The good and the bad, the benefits and the drawbacks, and the focus and the distractions are all worth it in the end; these will all benefit the improved *Built for Global* outcome that follows.

Built Trust In-Country

One Country, Many Cultures

Especially the first time, expanding a business in the global marketplace is fraught with a variety of challenges. One major challenge is the establishment of trust with local partners, intermediaries, clients, and government agencies. Stories of challenging projects are commonplace, but so are the accounts of impressive achievements that have come from an enlightened approach to overseas market entry and perseverance.

You are bringing your products and services into *their* country. What follows is a compelling account of a project that illustrates the importance of understanding cross-cultural values and principles—a critical step toward the establishment of trust between all parties. Without that cross-cultural understanding, trust is virtually impossible to achieve.

A Story over Coffee with Daniel Turner

Daniel Turner was contracted to represent an American IT company during the implementation of a national infrastructure project in Kuwait. The project's ambitious goal was to simultaneously modernize and integrate the management of telecommunications, gas, electricity, water, sewage, and property rights throughout the country. This was a project that would be valued at well over $100 million USD in today's currency.

The Kuwaiti government wanted, and could afford to acquire, the best-of-the-best in IT products and services from around the world, including

* *German precision in specification,*
* *Japanese meticulous project management, and*
* *American innovative technology.*

The project was multinational from the outset. The Kuwaitis commissioned a German consulting firm to write the project specifications. The project specs were distributed globally for bids by multinationals from North America, Europe, and Asia. A large Japanese corporation was selected to be the main contractor, and predictably its bid included a supply of Japanese technologies. The Kuwaiti government, however, stipulated that it would only accept the bid with computer-related technology supplied from a particular US company.

It is reasonably accurate to say that the tribal-based Kuwaiti culture respects power founded on a tightly trusted inner circle. Kuwaiti trust is rarely extended beyond that closely connected group unless there is genuine, time-tested admiration, respect, and empathy for an outsider.

On the other hand, Japanese management is highly collaborative, soliciting the participation of many people. The Japanese extend and build trust over time, through experienced-based relationships and "keiretsu" *loyalties.*

American management style (on the surface at least) offers trust relatively quickly to business partners and collaborators, until such time as that trust is damaged or lost. The American approach allows for rapid decision-making, but at a much higher level of risk than is acceptable to the Kuwaiti or Japanese business cultures.

In addition to the participation of the German engineers, the Japanese contractor, and the US technology supplier, a Polish firm was contracted to do the cartography (mapmaking), an Indian workforce was employed for middle management and data gathering, and a Palestinian group was responsible for data entry. And, of course, Kuwaiti nationals provided overall project management on behalf of their government. This national infrastructure project had become truly multinational, implemented with the help of organizations from seven very different cultures.

Risks at the early stages of the project were perceived as manageable by all parties; political relations between Kuwait and the United States were good, English was the accepted language for conducting business, and Kuwait valued US technology-related products and services.

Daniel was the project manager and systems consultant for the US technology supplier. He felt comfortable and confident with the multicultural team. Because the company's technology was such a large component of the overall project, Daniel decided (with end-client insistence) to move to Kuwait for what was to be a five-year commitment. All the major pieces seemed to be in place.

In Kuwait, the path ahead quickly became mired in cross-cultural misunderstandings and conflicts. There was a lack of trust between the different organizations involved in the project.

For the project to be a success on all sides, trust had to be built between the Kuwaiti government, the Japanese contractor, and Daniel's company. The variation in management styles between these very different cultures was astonishing, especially given the world's progress toward a widely integrated, global economy.

Ongoing project difficulties and the lack of cultural understanding seemed overwhelming. At one point it threatened to shatter the entire project. About halfway into the project, the issue of financial penalties arose, as delivery delays were significant. This incident coincided with what was probably the low point of the whole project. Millions of dollars in progress payments owed to the Japanese contractor were suddenly blocked by the Kuwaiti government based on contractual benchmarks agreed upon prior to the start of the project. In response, the Japanese contractor flew a delegation of senior executives halfway around the world to Kuwait to address the issue of financial penalties.

The date, time, and location were set for the meeting. As is custom (and obligation) in Japan, the Japanese executives arrived on time.

Kuwaiti management, as is often customary, arrived late. As the clock slowly ticked, there was concern among the Japanese executives that the Kuwaiti government officials might not show up at all, causing a critical rise in tension for the Japanese representatives (none of whom had any previous on-the-ground experience in the Middle East).

Finally, a top Kuwaiti manager arrived and immediately demanded an explanation of why the Japanese delegation was now in Kuwait. This was his way of starting a negotiation, aimed at strengthening his starting position. The Japanese interpreted his behavior and comments in a seriously different way.

Strangely enough, there are myths and legends told within both the Arab and Japanese cultures that would have helped each side to understand

and alleviate the situation. But, in the heat of the moment, literally and figuratively in the Kuwaiti summer, when temperatures climb above 100° Fahrenheit and with millions of dollars at stake (not to mention careers), the lessons of time-honored allegories are often overlooked.

At the request of the Kuwaiti government, Daniel Turner shifted into a more critical role. He was asked to help resolve the issues arising from the dysfunctional relationships between the Kuwaitis, the Japanese, and the Americans. The Japanese contractor had the most to lose if things got worse—and the most to gain if the project ultimately succeeded. The Kuwaiti government's request was based on a belief that Daniel was best positioned to work with all parties.

Daniel was "reassigned" to work with and for the Japanese contractor, rather that the US technology company because he had the trust of all parties.

Resolving the situation was a tall order. Daniel worked discreetly, never suggesting a "must do" solution, but slowly building cross-cultural understanding and the beginnings of interorganizational trust. He encouraged each culture to be receptive to the others, while using diplomacy to constructively align the different players. Much of Daniel's success came from getting the parties to understand the benefits of "making the project work" rather than remaining focused on the problems that had plagued the project in its early stages and placing blame.

In the end, the project was successful. The financial penalties were lifted, and the five-year project was completed on budget, within scope, and only six months over deadline, which all those involved considered to be as good as on time.

Daniel Turner has continued to achieve international success throughout a career that has taken him to virtually every corner of the world over a span of thirty years. He is an international business development specialist who helps companies of all sizes open new markets, resolve cross-cultural challenges, and achieve global targets. Check out Turner Global[32] *for more information.*

Trust is an asset that is much easier to lose than gain. Trust is critically important in most (if not all) global business relationships. But trust cannot occur without cross-cultural understanding that goes well beyond simply knowing how to shake hands or present a business card.

The punch line of the Kuwaiti project, as Daniel describes it, was that shortly after the completion of the project, Kuwait was invaded by Iraq. All of the project's IT resources were seized by Iraqi soldiers and transported in open-backed military trucks along the bumpy, sand-swept roads between Kuwait City and Baghdad, a journey of more than 350 miles. Large disk drives, data packs, state-of-the-art graphic workstations, and an array of VAX computers (previously housed in a pristine, temperature-controlled environment) arrived as nothing more than junk, to the great relief of the American parties concerned.

Business success is all about capturing customers. The first few innovators and early-adopter customers validate your business model, provide references, and initiate sales in-country. The next handful of early-adopter and early-majority customers build momentum and provide the traction you need. Beyond that you are looking to register market share in-country.

In taking a company into international markets, failure often occurs as a result of unrestrained enthusiasm and moving too fast. The excitement of capturing the first few innovators and early adopters in one country leads to initiating sales in adjacent countries before firmly establishing the primary market. If expansion is done before "crossing the chasm," the result is often failure.

The process roughly follows the technology adoption lifecycle that Geoffrey Moore outlines in his book *Crossing the Chasm.*[33] While it is challenging to find and attract those first few innovators and early adopters, the truly difficult step is capturing the early majority. This is the chasm where many companies fail—unable to capture that next, all-important handful of customers to build momentum. Moore focuses more on disruptive or discontinuous technology developments, but the underlying message is the same: focus on one group at a time. Begin with the innovators, then the early adopters, the early majority, the late majority, and finally the laggards.

The bridge of trust needs to be built between the initial customers and market expansion.

What's in it for Customers?

Customers, whether individuals or companies, are people. Companies are just a collection of people with a common business goal. People do things for all sorts of reasons.

If you don't know what prospective customers want, need, or value, you are in no position to sell them anything. As we discussed in chapter 2, "Add Value," if you understand the value gap and what's really behind the Four Whys, you can create momentum and capture market share quickly. Without the knowledge of in-country value and "why," you are likely to be pitching product features and attributes when customers really want to understand impact and outcome.

Buyer motivation can get pretty complicated. There is a lot of great thought leadership on what motivates buyers in sales classics such as *Strategic Selling*[34] and in more current books such as *Selling for Dummies*[35] and lots of *SPIN*[36] in between. Buyer reasons and motivation are a complex mix of personal and organizational stimulus. What follows are the six most common.

> *"This can solve my problem"* is a comment that indicates that the customer has identified a problem and has determined that your offering will address it (filling the gap). This brings to mind a classic consumer

example: "I have the headache, and you have the aspirin." Customers may already know they have a problem, or they may be clueless, and you will have to educate them. Education takes time, so consider that in your marketing plan and sales-cycle time estimates.

"There's pot of gold at the end of that rainbow" is an indicator of a customer motivated by payback or extreme desire. The customer perceives that purchasing your stuff will result in a high-level outcome (this could be wealth, power, social standing, image, or something else). In a B2B sale, this might be the desire to build company profits or revenue. Many business and personal productivity tools may be purchased with this motivator—health and wellness products too.

"If we don't act now, we will be in trouble." Fear sells. Fear sells everything from cleaning products and bottled water to cybersecurity. The potential of negative consequences motivates these customers. There is a tremendous amount of advertising invested to protect us from real or perceived threats. Sometimes, it is the fear of missing that "once in a lifetime opportunity." For B2B sales it could be fear that the competition will capitalize on it first. For consumer products it's worry, uncertainty, and self-doubt about everything from cleanliness to safety to longevity.

"That rocks" is a sign that the person finds pleasure a key motivator. In consumer "feel-good" products and services, it's easy to see how vacation travel, home décor, and hobbies appeal. When Apple introduced the first iPhone, it wasn't a better cell phone than number-one Nokia, but the user interface and user experience was exceptional. It delighted customers because it *rocked*! Within five years Apple was number one, and Nokia had slipped off the radar.[37] In any industry or any economy, luxury-class items can be positioned with this motivator.

"This really looks good" is a sign that image or vanity may be driving the buying decision. This drives everything from brand image to beauty and sustainability. These customers are drawn by affinity and the desire

to be connected with something that provides a positive image; Apple's iPhone has capitalized on this desire as well. In B2B, this motivation can drive solar energy purchases, wastewater treatment, and "green" projects. In consumer goods it can be as simple as making people feel good and look good. It's what fuels the more than $65 billion cosmetics industry![38]

"Everyone else is doing it; we should too" is a remark that identifies classic follow-the-leader purchasers. When the trend is your friend, things can work in your favor for both B2B and consumer products. We talked about the importance of catching a wave in chapter 2, in "Is the Trend Your Friend?" The media, high-profile personalities, industry analysts, and social media drive follow-the-leader behavior.

Why customers buy is a complex mixed bag of reasons and motivators. The better you can understand the potential customer's motivation to purchase, the more effectively you will be able to penetrate the new market.

Prove Your Value

Accelerator for success: "under promise and over deliver" is the best advice for building trust and achieving a high level of customer satisfaction. There exists no better way to build trust with customers than to *prove* the value of your products or services by extending a proof-of-concept offer.

Customer agreements for proof of concept (PoC) have four major variations: money-back guarantee, contingent purchase, pilot, and trial.

* *Money-back guarantee:* Customer pays for the product and services at the time of purchase and is given a window of time to return the products for a full refund if not satisfied. The reason for return can be subjective ("if not completely satisfied") or objective (such as nonperformance). This PoC approach is best for low-cost products and consumer goods.

* *Contingent purchase:* Conditional purchase of products and services based on achieving a mutually agreeable success criteria. Typically, there is no money paid up front, but the purchase agreement has been executed, and your company will generate an invoice on a specific date or when certain benchmarks are achieved.

* *Pilot:* Customer agrees to pay for a portion of the installation in advance with the remaining payment due upon successful completion of the PoC pilot. In effect, this is a progress-payment approach with specific dates or benchmarks established to trigger payment. There is a clear expectation of success on behalf of the customer. Pilots are a great PoC for your US customers looking to use your products and services in a new country.

* *Trial or Freemium:* Customer receives PoC at no cost with no obligation to purchase. This requires a second sales process to convert the trial or freemium into a sale, which extends the time to close. If dates and success criteria have been established in advance, that will reduce the time to close. If significant features are not in the freemium, that encourages a more rapid conversion. Our experience is that trials extend beyond their original dates and take significant additional effort to close. Freemium to premium conversion rates vary by industry and may be lower than expected, as customers often choose to opt out or "make do" with the freemium version.

Robert and Janet prefer both pilots and contingent-purchase agreements because all the details for a successful close are complete before the PoC begins. Freemium offerings can be successful for software, apps, and other products or services that scale.

Money-back guarantees work well in consumer markets or for low-cost items but are less desirable in B2B or high-ticket-item sales.

Trials are Robert and Janet's least favorite because a trial requires two complete sales cycles, which slows the process down tremendously; the first close is for the PoC, and the second close is for the final purchase.

Whatever option you choose, make it a win-win-win for the customer, your company, and the mountain guide.

No matter how you approach a PoC, if possible try to have your company's time and expenses covered. **The goal of a PoC is not making money but rather building trust, validating your value proposition, and building a customer reference base.** Try to cover basic costs, in whole or part, and not lose your shirt in the process.

The PoC process has four primary tasks:

1) Set goals and objectives.
2) Prepare for customer contact.
3) Go sell something.
4) Monitor PoC delivery for success.

Your first proof-of-concept customers are early adopters, willing to take a risk on your offering, which is unproven in-country. See appendix 5, "Tasks for a Successful PoC," for more detail.

Stephanie works for Alex at TolpaTek and is based in Philadelphia. Stephanie and her team specialize in a unique TolpaTek product set with a typical US sales cycle of thirty days. When opening up the market in Spain, Stephanie and her team discovered that it took significantly longer to prospect, qualify, and close PoC customers in Spain. In fact, to sell the PoC took three-months—three times longer than selling a PoC in the United States. Thank goodness the mountain guide, Javier, was already in place, or it probably would have taken longer.

Stephanie made five trips to Spain to sell the PoC during that three-month period—one with Alex and two with a sales engineer (SE). Stephanie also decided to establish demo capabilities in-country, which required some customization and could serve as backup images for the PoCs. The initial outlay was higher than usual, in part because of the number of plane tickets, but Stephanie knew it as a worthwhile investment to get Spain kicked off to a good start.

OOPS! Forgot to mention that Stephanie also drove finance and OA (order administration) crazy with new agreements and a new currency, the euro. Once the first PoC deal was inked, Stephanie set the home team into action. Good news: it turned out that exporting wasn't difficult. In the United States, preparing for a PoC only took about a week, but in Spain it took almost thirty days.

The original PoC run time was an agreed thirty-day pilot, but Stephanie had to extend it twice. There were a variety of reasons for the extensions: technical issues, local holidays, and other items that were good for customer relations. Thus, thirty days turned into three months!

What would normally be a PoC investment of sixty to ninety days in the US market took a full eight months when launching operations in Sain!

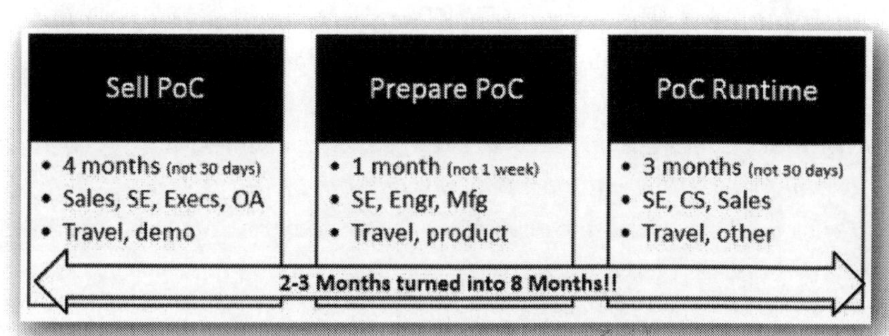

Figure 21: Expect proof-of-concept extensions

Stephanie had to explain this to Alex and the CEO, and the first-year sales projections for Spain had to be revised downward. Luckily, everyone understood that this was part of the learning experience. You can learn from Stephanie's experience.

It will take longer than you expect. Set reasonable, low-to-moderate expectations so you don't miss targets and have to "explain it" later to your boss. **Opening a new country, expect the initial sales cycle to take two to four times longer than the normal sales cycle—and sometimes more.** Tom Peters, coauthor of *In Search of Excellence*, has it right: under promise and over deliver. The good news for Stephanie was that the PoC was successful, so it provided a great launching pad into Spain, then Portugal, and later into other European countries.

The first proof-of-concept customers are invaluable to your company. PoCs assess and validate a wide variety of things important to your continued success in-country. The PoCs check off a variety of key issues and answer vital questions:

- ✓ Are design changes required for operability?
- ✓ What's important to selling the product/service in-country?
- ✓ What's important to buyers?
- ✓ Can we establish in-country market credibility?
- ✓ Do you understand market requirements?
- ✓ Have you identified a low- risk investment strategy for this market?

Being a proof-of-concept customer is valuable to the customer:

- ✓ It solves a problem that was previously unsolvable.
- ✓ It gives them an edge in their marketplace.
- ✓ It provides economic benefit for the customer or his or her business.
- ✓ Workflow may improve.
- ✓ It helps leverage global capabilities not previously available.
- ✓ It provides low-risk improvement to personal or business operations.

Get Noticed

When entering a new country, develop a strategy that will get you into the market. You need to be noticed and recognized and build awareness. Customers want to know that your company offering is now an option in-country.

Enlist the assistance of your mountain guide and your marketing department. Don't be afraid to ask for help. Marketing is expert at setting up marketing campaigns. Your mountain guide understands the unique characteristics. Be clear about what you want to accomplish.

The initial "getting noticed" plan should be extremely focused, require only a small budget, integrate with face-to-face activities, be hands-on, and speak without you.

Accelerate "getting noticed" success by starting with the end in mind. The goal of "getting noticed" is to find proof-of-concept customers so that you and the mountain guide can close them. The first customers are innovators and early adopters. Laser focus your marketing messages to attract customers willing to partner with you in-country to prove local value and to be first movers.

Sip; don't guzzle. Keep your budget small. You are trying to get noticed by a select group of early adopters. This is not a comprehensive integrated marketing plan, which will come later when the in-country market has been validated.

Integrate the "getting noticed" plan with face-to-face meetings. People and businesses in the United States are willing to buy from people they don't know, but **the rest of the world works F2F** (face-to-face). The people you will be working with want to get to know you personally, build mutual trust, and connect with your personal commitment. Your mountain guide can help direct construction of a successful F2F "getting noticed" plan.

Face-to-face meetings with prospective customers is a top priority, whether one-on-one or one-on-many. Private shows for an exclusive audience will generally yield good results, if you can get enough people in the room. The audience may be smaller, but all of its attention will be on your company and your offerings. Ask members of the press, industry watchers, or media specialists to attend; nothing better than a little free press coverage! Quite often the US Embassy in-country will help to organize a private event, depending on the type of product or service that you are selling.

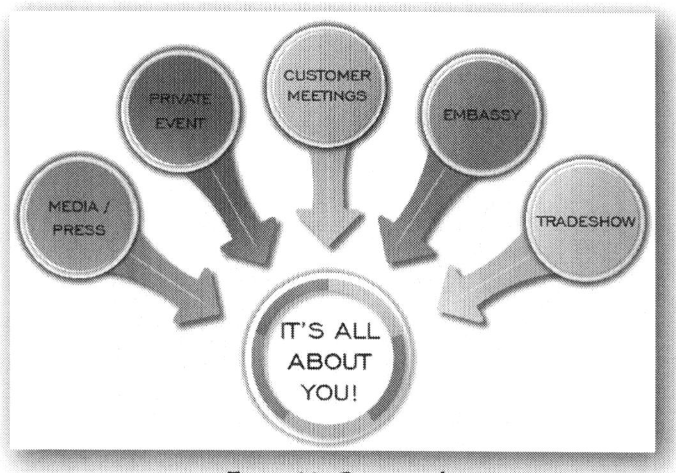

Figure 22: Get noticed

Trade shows can be a good market introduction, but getting noticed will be diluted by other companies also vying for attention. Have your mountain guide suggest and help orchestrate events.

Leveraging press and media outside the United States can play an important role in your "getting noticed" plan. At minimal cost, it can provide big impact. Article marketing, press releases, and well-placed thought-leadership pieces can help build awareness and interest. Visit newspaper offices (newspapers are still vital communication tools outside the United States), especially if your company has good industry recognition. Coordinate media interviews for visiting executives or experts.

B2C companies should always develop a social-media marketing plan. The United States is not the only connected country; 77 percent of Twitter and 83 percent of Facebook users[39] reside outside the United States. If your customers are looking to social media for answers, don't let them down. B2B, B2P, and B2G companies should also develop a social-media plan appropriate to their industry.

Consider the timing of your activities. Launch your offerings in harmony with local business process, seasons, and customs. Business cycles, buying cycles, and life cycles affect the ebb and flow of business. This is simple stuff that won't be a **speed bump** with a little attention.

December is summer in Chile, and you might not get the attention of decision-makers during summer break and Christmas in this predominately Christian country. Monsoon season in parts of India, mostly around July, makes transportation difficult. With annually shifting dates of observation, the celebration of Ramadan and Hari Raya in Muslim countries such as Malaysia might make purchasing agents less available to hear your story. Rely on the expertise of your mountain guide to help you select the right time to best leverage business cycles in-country.

Here are five of Robert's best practices for successful "getting noticed" meetings:

* **Don't skimp on preparation.** Prepare in advance for F2F meetings by sending out an agenda and reminders. Ask for input into the topics to be covered, but set the agenda yourself.

* **Establish a two-way relationship** from the beginning. Ask the person or company visited to present first; it is a show of respect and will also help to fill in knowledge gaps for you. If the others decline, Robert has found that it is often an indicator that the relationship will

not be balanced or win-win. Allow a lot of time for discussion. Expect meetings to begin with ten minutes of small talk and introductions. If it is a sixty-minute meeting, limit structured comments to twenty minutes and allow for twenty to thirty minutes for open, two-way discussion.

* **Demonstrate commitment.** Although English is the language of business in most countries, a presentation in English, coupled with a simple collateral piece in the local language, illustrates your commitment to the market. Or you could take your English presentation and have it translated. A leave-behind printed copy of your presentation including both English and local language will get circulated. In China, Japan, or Korea, localized business cards in kanji give an extra kick. Your presentation and collateral can both be in English; ask your mountain guide for best practices.

* **Make show-and-tell relevant.** Ask your mountain guide to present a product demonstration or show-and-tell, if appropriate, in the local language and with local stories. It will resonate more deeply with the customer. Product demonstrations in local language provide a subtle illustration that your product has already made the transition to in-country use.

* **Show gratitude.** Gifts are customary in many places around the world. Gifts should be something small, unique, and meaningful, branded with your company logo if appropriate, but not necessarily expensive. Always send a personalized thank-you note after a meeting, via e-mail or snail mail. Ask your mountain guide for best practices. In many Asian countries, it's not about what the gift is—it's about how beautifully it is wrapped!

Devise a strategy to get noticed in your new market. Focus on the fundamentals. Consider the right time and the right place and maybe even a power play. Enter with some excitement.

Business 101

The customer is king…or queen…or the royal family.

Even if you don't believe it, your customers believe it's true. So, treat them like royalty.

Accelerate the sales process by treating customers like royalty. A well-defined sales process respects the customers' buying process. It maps to the customers' needs as they traverse their decision-making process and assists them as they evaluate your offer and investigate options. Customers want to make a good decision that they can live with. **A well-defined sales process builds trust.**

Start with the US sales process as outlined in sales force automation (SFA) or customer relationship management (CRM) (consult websites such as Salesforce.com or SugarCRM.com). Review the process in detail with your mountain guide and ask him or her to point out local considerations or differences. A typical B2B sales process in the United States looks something like this five-step process.

Figure 23: Typical B2B sales process

The many sales tools and techniques that have made your company successful in the United States are a great starting point. But, expect the process to be a bit different as you enter a new country. Your mountain guide will help evaluate the process. As you build experience in-country, it will help validate what works most effectively. You want to localize the sales process:

* **Prospect.** Hand select prospective PoC customers by name when you are getting started. Leverage contacts in the mountain guide's business network; personal introductions are the best point of entry.

* **Create need.** Perhaps it is not so much creating as it is discovering need. It's important to understand how the need for your offering is viewed locally. Are customers fully aware of their needs, or is some local education required? In-country prospects may have problems that can be solved by your product but be unaware of the existence of a solution. Conversely, they may not even know that they have a problem. Do customers see your offering as a priority when compared with other important local issues? Is there a sense of urgency that makes a customer want to act now?

* **Write a MOU.** The usage of a memorandum of understanding (MOU) is very common outside the United States. An MOU is something like a concept proposal, providing a "use case" outlining how their business will use your products or services and will benefit. An MOU is used internally by your customer to confirm understanding and build internal sponsorship to move forward. It is nonbinding and indicates your intentions to do business together. An MOU is also used externally. Issued as a press release, it provides important visibility for your relationship, your value proposition, and your company. Appendix 6 contains a more detailed description of MOUs.

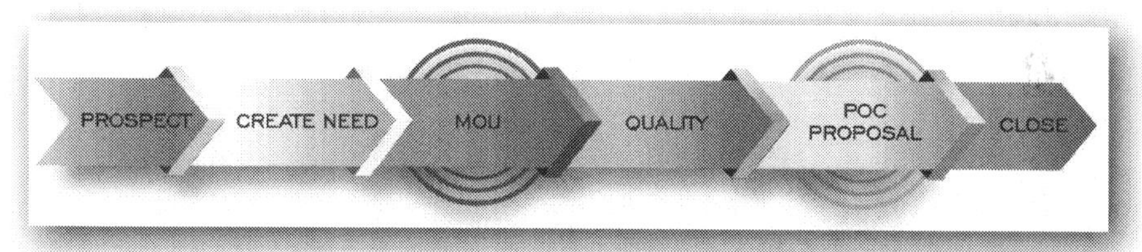

Figure 24: Typical international B2B sales process

* **Qualify customers.** As with any sales process, qualifying the customer happens at every stage. Does the customer have the willingness and ability to buy? Have you made contact with someone who has the authority to buy? Authority to make buying decisions will be different from what occurs in the United States. Be sure there is a real need for your product and that the prospective customer has money to pay for it. If you don't do this early, you could spend valuable time and resources chasing somebody's dream that turns into your nightmare.

* **Present the PoC Proposal.** Robert and Janet's experience in other countries is that proposals are often presented as two separate documents. One document contains specific technical and implementation details of what you are offing for a specific project. The second document contains pricing and terms. The reason for two separate documents is that they will have two different audiences for review and approval. This dual-document approach lends itself well to proof-of-concept proposals. The technical details are the technical details; the pricing and terms outline the PoC duration, success criteria, and payment terms.

* **Close.** Negotiate and close. It's the start of a long-term business relationship and your entry in-country.

It's not a one-size-fits-all world. Your sales process in the United States gives you a great head start, but expect local variations for every country. Spain will be different from Italy, and Europe will be different from India.

Assess the Depth of Trust

① Building Home-Team Trust

1. What is your vision and your mission? What are your goals in taking the company to its next stage of international expansion? Write it down.

   It could be something simple like this: *"Make (your company) a (pioneer / break-through / leading) player in (whatever you do) in (x country / y region you are targeting)."*

2. Evaluate the strength commitment you have from key departments or key players in these departments. You are taking the company into

new international markets, and you will need their help and support. Is their commitment weak, neutral, or strong?

* finance—commitment to new currency, tariffs, order processing, and more
* engineering—commitment to technical adaptation and compliance
* product marketing—commitment to product changes and localization
* marketing—commitment to positioning, messaging, and promotion in-country
* customer support—commitment to addressing time-zone and in-country needs
* CEO and the management team—commitment for strategic alignment

3. Assess who's in the boat paddling with you and who wants to sink your boat.

    * List the top three positive influencers.

      ____
      ____
      ____

    * List the three biggest *Monsieur Saboteurs*.

      ____
      ____
      ____

    * Identify three influential players who are neutral today but whom you want to get on your team.

      ____
      ____
      ____

Assessment Action Plan: Develop a plan for each of the three categories of home-team players. Enlist the four Cs: communication, consensus, collaboration, and clarity.

* What actions can you take to keep positive influencers committed, enthusiastic, and helping your efforts?

* What can you do to change Monsieur Saboteur's opinion or position? Maybe he or she has incorrect or insufficient information. Could there be a perception of personal or organizational risk that needs to be addressed? Maybe there is even a bit of professional jealousy. Could it be fear of the unknown? If you can't change Monsieur Saboteur's position, look for how to neutralize it or minimize the collateral damage.

* What activities can positively involve neutral players? How can you get them in the boat? Perhaps your positive influencers can help with this.

② Building Customer Trust

1. What is your "getting noticed" plan? What's in the plan? What's not in the plan? What needs more investigation? The plan might cover

    * one-on-one customer meetings,
    * trade show(s),
    * private events,
    * demonstrations,
    * an embassy event,
    * media/Press, and
    * other.

2. What is your company's sales process in the United States today? Surely it is documented somewhere: in CRM, sales training, marketing plan, somewhere. Find out about stages, entry/exit criteria, stage duration, and more. If your sales process is not documented, it's time to do it!

3. If you are currently selling outside the United States, how does the sales process vary from country to country? If the sales process outside the United States hasn't been documented, it's time to get that done. Ask the people selling outside the country to do this for you. It will be an invaluable starting place to determine the variations necessary for the new country you plan to enter.

4. What type of proof of concept do you and your mountain guide think will be most effective in-country? Why?

   - ☐ money-back guarantee
   - ☐ contingent purchase
   - ☐ pilot
   - ☐ trial
   - ☐ other: ______________________________
   - ☐ PoC is not required

5. Leverage your prior experience. Where has your company used this proof-of-concept methodology previously, and what was the outcome?

   * duration or cycle time
   * close rate
   * customer retention

Chapter 6

Are You Going Global?

The applause thundered and seemed to last forever, although it was only a few priceless seconds. Time seemed to stand still in that moment. All eyes were on him as the audience applauded and cheered. But, it wasn't just him, it was him and the team. Alex remembered those treasured moments in little league or in high school track when he crossed that finish line. This time was different. He stood on a platform above the New York Stock Exchange when TolpaTek went public.

That was a lot of years ago now, but the amazing feeling hadn't faded. Alex was proud to have been a key part of the TolpaTek team, then and now. TolpaTek's growth came from opening new markets in the United States, and the company now was expanding internationally. A number of inquiries were coming in from Southeast Asia. Alex decided to enter the Southeast Asian market via Singapore. There was no language barrier because English is the language of business in Singapore, although modifications were required to meet industry regulatory requirements. In the first two years, TolpaTek added many new customers and was able to serve multinational customers; this allowed the company to become visible in Southeast Asia. The rate of return exceeded TolpaTek's goals.

The market in Singapore was stable (not growing or declining), and TolpaTek was able to establish a profitable business that supported its own operations. This profitable base provided a platform to explore other Southeast Asian markets. TolpaTek started selling in Australia and the Philippines to multinational companies where "English-speaking" products were acceptable (compounding).

As the business foundation grew, Alex was able to expand the business into India, New Zealand, and Pakistan (more compounding). Wise investment helped TolpaTek achieve a strong rate of return and build for global by compounding its investment to open new markets.

Are You the One?

What does it take to be successful in international business? Robert and Janet are often asked, "What is the profile of the person who will be successful?" The purpose of *Built for Global* is to make success in international business more of a science than an art. Anyone can do it; however, there are a few traits that will elevate your opportunity for success.

Desire. Are you driven? You have to want it. Wanting to succeed internationally will exponentially increase your odds of success. Do you want to travel? Do you really enjoy it? Can you see your CV or résumé with a global spin?

A true international business leader will take action, find out a way to make things work, and won't quit. These special individuals will find a way to work through the challenges and will give it everything they've got.

Leadership. Do you have a clear and compelling vision? Contagious optimism and vision will energize others to join your team. Someone who is perhaps a little overoptimistic can see past the speed bumps in the road. Can you visualize what success looks like, even if you don't yet know how to make it happen?

> Leaders want to run with the ball and will inspire others to drive for the goal line. They are both optimistic and practical. Leadership is fundamental to de-risking opportunity, a willingness to tackle tough issues head on. International business leaders are willing to forge ahead on their own, yet eager to ask for help and build a team.

Crossover. Can you move across boundaries—cross functionally, cross industry, cross-culturally? Do you see connections between seemingly diverse elements that others miss? Do you look for commonality or dissimilarity? Do you see links or gaps? Do you make uncommon connections that yield new and interesting results? Do you embrace solutions outside your comfort zone?

> Highly successful international business leaders are nonconformists; they will make atypical connections feel familiar and comfortable. It is this ability to cross over that can make the value connection within new markets. They have long-range vision, a unique kind of flexibility, peripheral vision, and open-mindedness. They can work comfortably across organizational lines, span a variety of industries, and traverse cultures with ease.

Integrity. You must, at heart, be honest, reliable, and truthful—a person who does not lie or cheat others and who is honest with yourself. Are you genuine and authentic? Do you keep promises that you make to yourself and to others? Do you stand by your principles?

> Integrity is the foundation for building and keeping trust. It is being true to yourself and to others that you are working with. The successful international business leader will do the right thing, even if it is difficult, leaving bias and personal interest aside.

Attitude

Think positively. Visualize success. Solve problems quickly. It's the same with any human endeavor: you have to have the right attitude. It's what got you where you are in your career. Attitude is also a bit brash and cocky but not arrogant and boastful. It's why you are taking your company global, whether this is your first foray outside the United States or just another country to add to your global-expansion checklist.

Don't look at the rock: look at the path around the rock. Every mountain biker or motorcycle rider knows that if you look at the rock, you will hit the rock. The "dominant thought" principal[40] says we travel in the direction of our most dominant thoughts. Think positively, and you will navigate around the rocks in the path of your global success. Think negatively, and you will slow down your global journey, hitting rocks along the way.

Your attitude will help you attract a home team, mountain guide, partners, and customers. Your attitude will help you look beyond short-term obstacles and setbacks. Obvious? Yes, it is. Positive thinking is not a new concept; this is merely a reminder. Positive thinking is ancient history and yet still trending now.

Can you see it? Do you have a vision for what success looks like in the country you are entering? This is about your goals and objectives over time. But, there's more. Can you see it? Can you see in-country adoption? How your products and services improve personal, professional, or economic value for business, industry, government, and the people of the country you are entering? Can you really visualize your international success?

Invest

Built for Global is invested in your international success. What are *you* investing? You have to invest in order to grow. If you want to expand your business, your company, your brand, your customer base, and your value, it will take investment.

Should your company invest a little or a lot? The answer to that question depends on your goals. Throughout *Built for Global*, we talk about goals, objectives, vision, or outcome. We believe that every successful human endeavor requires some sort of aim or purpose. What would happen if a football team didn't know it needed to score the most points to win? Or what if a golfer didn't know that the lowest number of strokes wins the emblemed blazer and the big cash prize?

It's a classic risk-return tradeoff.[41] The basic principle is that potential return rises with an increase in risk. Low levels of uncertainty (lower risk) are associated with lower potential returns. Inversely, higher levels of uncertainty (higher risk) are associated with higher potential returns. The definition is valid, but only to a point. Embrace our four big concepts of value, de-risk, a mountain guide, and trust to improve your potential return. What's important is to find the right balance between risk and return for you and your company.

How much do you want to grow your business and how quickly? If you want to double the size of your current business in three to five years, expect to invest up to 50 percent of the current annual budget over that three- to five-year time span. If you are looking for incremental growth, then a lesser investment will be appropriate.

What is your risk tolerance? Risk of loss can be a multidimensional question. There could be loss of capital invested in a new market. There could be loss of valuable intellectual effort, redirected from current successful markets to unknown and unproven markets. There could be risk of underinvesting and competitors taking over the new market.

How much capital are you willing to risk? Budget for the first six months with contingency plans for the next twelve, eighteen, or twenty-four months. Don't expect big sales in the first year. Expect small sales to your proof-of-concept customers that will set the foundation for future sales.

Invest with purpose. Invest to rapidly validate business assumptions. Invest to quickly prove market traction. Spend that initial investment to reduce, minimize, or eliminate areas of risk. Find your balance. Look to answer questions that will help make better decisions of where to invest in the future. Entering a small market may require the same level of investment as entering a large potential market. A wiser approach may be to invest in the larger market first. Or your detective work may uncover that it is a better approach to enter the small market first and test your assumptions, before going big in the larger market.

Using an investment strategy as an analogy is a pretty powerful parallel. When investing your own money, you will consider the rate of return and the power of compounding. It's the same when investing in international markets.

* You want a market with the potential for a high **rate of return** that has the potential to increase over time. Invest in a market where your market penetration and market share can grow over time.

* If the market is also growing, that contributes to the **power of compounding in-country**. The power of compounding is realized when the business in-country becomes self-sustaining; in-country profits support in-country operations and fund future growth.

* The **power of compounding markets** is entering a country that becomes a gateway to other markets. For instance, you might enter Germany, which opens the European market or enter Malaysia, which opens Southeast Asia. The power of compounding is realized when one country becomes the success story that creates demand in similar or surrounding markets.

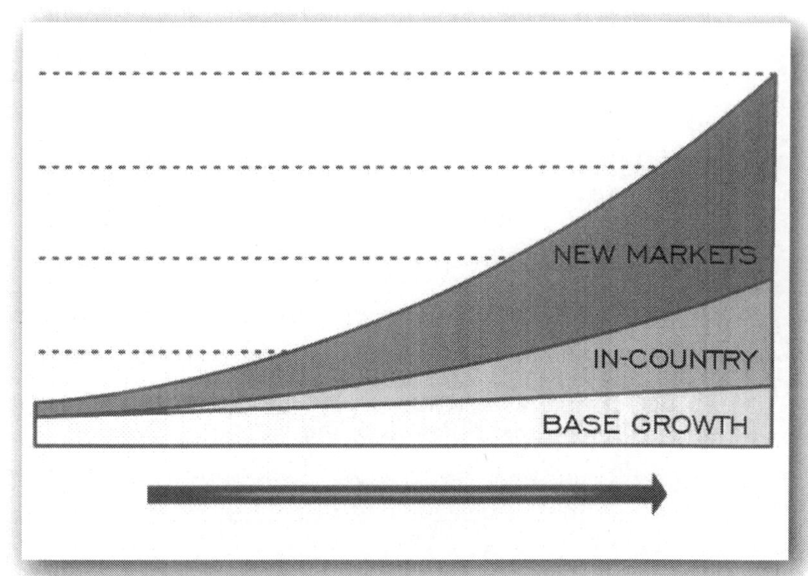

Figure 25: The magic of compounding

There are dangers when investing, whether it's your own money or your company's resources. You can avoid the common investment mistakes if you are aware of them. Here are some common investment mistakes.[42]

* **Mistake 1: Doing nothing.**
  There is no guarantee that you will be successful when entering a new market. But one thing is guaranteed: doing nothing will yield nothing.

* **Mistake 2: Starting late.**
  Delaying international expansion and letting competition establish a position can make your international growth plan more difficult and more expensive. There is a link between large scale and first movers.

* **Mistake 3: Investing without ample capital.**
  There are two concerns here. Can your company afford to take capital out of the core business? Are you investing enough capital in the new market to achieve your goals? Can you afford to invest?

* **Mistake 4: Short-term thinking.**
  It's a marathon, not a sprint. Are you willing and able to invest over a long period of time? Building for global is not like flipping a light switch on or off. You want to turn up the brightness over time.

* **Mistake 5: Playing it safe.**
  Do your homework, but don't get stuck in analysis paralysis. You may end up starting late or doing nothing at all. Heads up. Eyes open. You can turn a moving vehicle; you cannot turn one that is stationary.

* **Mistake 6: Playing it scary.**
  Do your homework. Do the due diligence. De-risk. There is no need to be a daredevil. Understand the risks and assess what you are reasonably willing to take on. Remember that the reputation you are putting on the line is the company's, as well as your own.

Some Companies Choose *Not* to Go Global

As important as it is to decide what you *are* going to do, it is just as important to decide what you are *not* going to do. All companies have limited resources. It is important to focus limited resources on the most important priorities.

There are many reasons that companies choose *not* to go global. Some of these are legitimate, and some are just excuses. There is a lot of gray matter that goes into these decisions, and the justifications may be equally gray, making it difficult to distinguish between rational and irrational reasons. No matter what the decision, go or no-go, taking the business international has risk.

Common reasons (excuses?) that companies choose *not* to go global include the following:

* language barriers
* unfamiliar cultural practices and etiquette

* unknown local laws and politics
* limitation of foreign labor laws
* concerns it will be time-consuming and complex
* added expense of travel and establishing a presence
* difficulties finding a partner (or partners) that can be trusted
* concerns about defocusing company resources

All of these reasons are valid. But all of these reasons can be addressed, and the risks can be minimized. In *Built for Global,* we address these common reasons, along with others, to help you determine which ones are valid concerns.

Never make the go / no-go decision on intuition or "gut-feel" alone. Do your homework. Chapter 3, "De-Risk," provides important considerations when determining whether taking your business to international markets is the right decision or not.

Another Story over Coffee with Janet Gregory

Janet worked with a company that had a CEO from India who maintained strong ties in-country and with entrepreneurs in the Indian diaspora. The trusted network was impressive. Despite this trusted base, India was not the best market for their international debut. The value proposition did not align with customer needs within India, and the market was not big enough at the time. Even a company with visionary leadership and strong international roots must do the proper market research before launching into a new market.

Yes, they speak a different language in many other countries. But even English is different in English-speaking countries such as Australia and the United Kingdom. It's not all bad: English is the accepted global language of business, and you can get by as English-only for a while. Your product and service offering probably has a language component that will need to be addressed as you explore market use, so be mindful of it.

Opening a new market, whether domestic or international, requires investment of resources, time, money, and key personnel. It is important to manage your expenses from the beginning, until you actually see traction. It can be instructive to use a successful domestic product introduction as a starting outline and guide for your international product launch. Go find the budget, product plan, initial projections, and actual results for that product introduction. There will be new questions that need to be asked and addressed, but there will also be many parallels.

One crucial key to success in taking your company international is that the entire company must support this important decision. Too often we hear "let the sales team check out the opportunity, and then we will decide what we want to do." Taking a company into international markets is not solely a sales effort. Executive travel will be required, finance will need to process orders in new currency, engineering and manufacturing will need to "localize" the product, customer service will need to provide support across time zones, and more. Every new international market exploration will require support of the entire team. You might even find some hidden assets in employees with language abilities and connections in other countries.

Your secret weapon is finding a mountain guide to steer you through the maze of local laws and customs. **Your mountain guide is the most essential component** of your international strategy. Finding a trusted partner (or partners) with key characteristics important to your success is *vital.*

The benefits exponentially outweigh the risks. We hope that you have found *Built for Global* interesting, entertaining and informative, helping you navigate into international waters.

If you choose *not* to enter an international market, that's okay. Make the decision for the right reasons, and be honest with yourself and with the business. It may be a NO decision today, *but* future factors may warrant a reevaluation to YES.

Go / No-Go

The goal of chapter 2, "Add Value," and chapter 3, "De-Risk" is to help you make an informed go / no-go decision. Evaluating and fine-tuning your value proposition along with researching vital data to de-risk your plan gives you the information necessary to make an informed decision. The go / no-go decision may also be time based. A "no-go" now does not preclude a "go" decision later on, when factors are more in your favor.

There is emotion in your decision. You are excited about the opportunity that has presented itself. You anticipate significant growth, personally, professionally, and organizationally. You are also concerned and maybe a bit anxious about the amount of travel required, the unknowns, and the possibility of failure.

There are facts that can be used to support your decision—either way. If you follow the simple, basic tenets in *Built for Global*, you have a foundation for making a good decision. Facts are facts. How do you sort through them to make a decision? Some facts may be obvious indicators, while others leave you questioning the right course of action.

Look for stability in your decision. Will the combination of decision factors, emotions, and facts result in sustainable success? Janet is a pilot and knows that a good landing requires a stable approach. She notes, "You have altitude, airspeed, and ideas; you don't want to run out of them at the same time." It's the same in business. Here are questions to consider as you make your decision:

* Is the economic and political climate stable? If you perceive risk in the next three to five years in economic and political conditions of a country, it may not be a good move for your company at this time.

* Is import/export activity predictable? If you anticipate country entry fraught with bureaucracy and regulatory hurdles, maybe it would be better to select a less problematic country for entry.

* How complex is the buying process? If it is difficult to identify where the money is coming from or how to get authorization for payment, maybe there are more predictable markets to pursue that will require less delay. You don't want to lengthen the decision process any more than necessary. If it is problematic getting money out of a country, consider an easier market for entry, until you are ready to assume the risk of a more complicated one.

Another Story over Coffee with Robert Pearlstein
Robert had to make a difficult go / no-go decision. Brazil was booming in education, robotics, and innovation. It looked like a great country for entry, based on stage of development and market. But, closer examination raised red flags; bureaucracy, difficulty identifying money, and getting money out of the country would hamper sales efforts. Robert turned his company's attention to South Korea and Scandinavia instead, where doing business was more straightforward. Brazil was off the radar for now but might be a viable option for the future when his organization might be better able to take the time necessary to establish operations.

It's a Marathon, Not a Sprint

It's a two-year marathon. Break it down into eight ninety-day sprints with goals, objectives, and milestones. Or think of it as a two-year contract you have entered into. How will the progress you are making be apparent to others? What are the benchmarks of advancement, movement, and development? Okay. Maybe it's a one-year or three-year marathon for you, but how will you prove value achieved?

Here's a high-level example of a two-year plan for a B2B tech company with a ninety-day sales-cycle time in the United States.

24 Month Plan for New Country Entry	90 Day Sprint Action Expectations
1st 90-day Sprint Training	• Mountain guide selected & on board • Value proposition documented • Competitive landscape figured out • Marketing minimums: website, collateral, presentation
2nd 90-day Sprint Start slow	• In-country prospect list identified • First customer meetings • Government meetings: requirements, incentives
3rd 90-day Sprint 9 months	• PoC prospects in the sales forecast • Validate pricing & value proposition • Plan for logistics, inventory & support
4th 90-day Sprint Half marathon	• Close & install first PoC customers • Pipeline for early customers, next year forecast • Logistics, installation, support process in place
5th 90-day Sprint Hit the wall	• First revenue, PoC converted to customers • Close first early customers • Case study, referrals, revamp marketing minimums
6th 90-day Sprint Get in stride	• Develop sales funnel • Add selling resources & demand creation efforts
7th 90-day Sprint Pick up pace	• Consistently build revenue run rate • Document sales process
8th 90-day Sprint Full stride	• Consistently build revenue run rate • First customer forum / user group in-country

Figure 26: Sample 24 month plan

How long does it take to successfully launch a new product in the United States with your proven partners, recognized brand, and competent fulfillment process? Remember that the same launch will take three or four times the cycle time in a new country where sales are unproven. If launching a new product into your existing established market takes six months to achieve a good run rate, expect a new international market to take eighteen to twenty-four months.

A sales-cycle time that's three or four times longer does not mean merely three or four trips to the country; your involvement and the involvement of your mountain guide demands three or four times the effort that a similar launch in the United States would require. It is not easy to build awareness, comprehension, understanding, and acceptance in a new country. You are not just launching a new product. **You are launching a company in a new country.** It's complex. It takes time.

A marathon runner starts slow and sets a manageable pace that he or she knows is manageable for twenty-six miles. The runner cannot sprint the whole race but can dig deep and break into a sprint when necessary. A seasoned runner knows that sprinting can overstress the body and induce the risk of "bonking," running out of internal resources and not finishing. The same goes for launching a business in a new country. The business can't sprint into the country. You need to start slow and set a manageable pace that you can stick to, even though your boss wants you to push harder.

The process will seem both fast and slow. There is a lot that you already know, because of your sales success in the United States. There will be days when incredible customer interest and sales are accelerating: the business "swoosh" that we love so much. Then there will be weeks that go by when nothing happens. There will be a constant tug-of-war between fast and slow as you enter a new country. The acceleration of new sales on one hand and longer sales cycles on the other.

It took ***years*** (perhaps decades) to build your US business to where it is today. If in twelve, eighteen, or twenty-four you can launch a business in a new country, that sounds pretty good, doesn't it?

When selling overseas, particularly in Asia, things will take longer than planned. Many Asian cultures have a group decision-making process; it takes longer than having a single decision-maker. Americans and Northern Europeans have a concept of "my food," for example. It's on my plate, and I decide what to do with it. In Asia, as well as many other parts of the world, food is shared, eaten from common plates. The business parallel is that Asians like to work out potential problems first and then make a deal. Americans and

Northern Europeans will agree on the deal first and then figure out how to address the problems.

We are goal-oriented, fast-moving salespeople just like you are. It's easy to want to make it all happen today. Push harder, work longer hours, set higher goals. We can wind ourselves up tighter and tighter. We believe. We have goals. That may work for a month or two—or maybe a quarter or two—but there will be casualties. Casualties on your home team, confirming that Monsieur Saboteur's suspicions were correct all along. Casualties on your away team—with your mountain guide, prospective partners, and prospective customers. Remember...those are real people on your home team and away team. They may not work the same way you do. You might even piss them off, and then they won't want to work with you. Don't be that guy or gal. It will only stress you out and everyone else around you.

Part of the process of building for global is having patience and helping the process unfold at the speed your company, and the new country, can handle. Set a manageable pace and stick to it. Then when you look back in twelve or eighteen months, you will be shocked to see how much you've accomplished.

Thank You

We can't thank you enough for making this journey with us. You've made it to the end of the book, but it's only the beginning! We hope we charged you with ideas and strategies for entering new markets and recharged your enthusiasm for navigating international business.

The world has changed. We live in a global economy, with global talent. Business opportunity lies within and without our borders. With a thoughtful approach to expanding your business outside of the United States, you can manage the complexity of going overseas and do it profitably with high standards.

The key is to do your homework, establish value, minimize risk, find guidance, and build trust in foreign markets as your business expands. To that end, we hope you find that our tools, methods, and practical ideas will help you compete and win!

Here are just a few final pieces of advice to leave you with to help you take our ideas and methods and shape them to fit your professional style. Form and mold them in a way that will keep you motivated.

✓ Connect with customers.
  * Make strong moves. Take small steps.

✓ Do your homework.
  * Plan your moves. Pick the space. Set your pace.

✓ Get a good mountain guide.
  * Find a mover and shaker that will be your navigator.

✓ Be a guardian.
  * Trust the process. Trust your team. Trust customers.
  * Trust can move mountains.

Make your move, and do it quickly! Move our ideas off these pages and make them yours. Put them into action because the world is moving fast. It may feel a bit awkward at first, but with your self-determination and sense of purpose, your skills will grow. It's how you got to where you are today and what will show you some amazing tomorrows.

You will survive drenching downpours, stifling heat waves, and bitter snowstorms. Conditions may not be ideal, but you have set out to achieve a goal. You have to *want it*, ***really*** *want it*, in order to drive yourself and your team to that finish line or the top of that mountain peak. Keep your vision clear; know the course, and avoid the cliffs. Stay nimble to dodge the rocks and be true to yourself.

Successful runners and hikers know that if they haven't taken time to train properly, they will pay for it on the race course or on the side of that mountain. For the best results, they have a vision of the goal, a drive to win, the flexibility to sidestep obstacles, and the integrity to persevere.

Good athletes listen to the advice of professionals who can help them learn. Though we cheer the individuals crossing the finish line, they each have a team supporting and motivating them along the way.

Build yourself, build your team, and build your company for global. Your CV or résumé will thank you for the experience, and you will create lifelong personal and professional friendships. Your team and company will thank you for expanding their horizons.

Success doesn't happen overnight. It will take time, so stay the course. Stay flexible and pivot to change direction when necessary. Expect to occasionally miss a step. Stay focused on your international goals. You can achieve meaningful personal and professional success in the global market.

More than anything, being successful in international business takes perseverance. Robert has run several half marathons, and Janet has climbed a number of interesting mountains. Taking your business international is the same—it is exciting, daunting, and will stretch you to the limits.

Small steps conquer miles, mountains, and new markets. Follow the steps outlined in this book, and you will be *Built for Global.*

Thank You!

About the Authors

This is Robert and Janet's first published work together.

Robert S. Pearlstein is vice president of global business development at SRI International. In this role, he cultivates opportunities with international corporate and government clients worldwide.

Robert has more than twenty years of experience building and executing go-to-market strategies for large enterprise companies as well as start-ups and emerging technology companies. He has extensive experience in international business development, market entry strategy, the venture capital funding process, large account strategic sales, and contract negotiation. Prior to joining SRI, Robert held senior executive positions for a variety of Silicon Valley venture backed companies and a large Japanese enterprise. His experience spans the B2B and Internet B2C domains. Robert received his MBA from Thunderbird, he completed the AEA executive management program at Stanford University, is fluent in English, Japanese, and Spanish. For more detail, find Robert's profile on LinkedIn: www.linkedin.com/in/robert-pearlstein-9766283/

Janet A. Gregory is cofounder and principal of Kickstart Alliance (www.kickstartall.com), a consulting firm dedicated to connecting clients with customers. She runs the business expansion practice for KickStart Alliance, providing strategy in business development and sales planning, assisting clients in developing existing markets as well as entering new ones.

Janet has over twenty-five years of corporate experience in Silicon Valley. The two most recent companies were successful startups; both resulted in successful IPOs. One was a turnaround, and for the other, Janet was a member of the founding executive team. In both startups Janet was vice president of sales taking them to profitability and dramatic year-over-year sales growth. Prior, Janet worked for two companies where she held multiple positions in business development, sales, and product marketing, rising from individual contributor to general manager. For more detail, find Janet's profile on LinkedIn: www.linkedin.com/in/janetg123

Appendix 1

Resources and References

Lots of great books to read. Here are a few we recommend.

* Curtis Carlson and William Wilmot, *Innovation: The Five Disciplines for Creating What Customers Want.*
* J. Michael Gospe, *The Marketing High Ground.*
* Frank Lavin and Peter Cohan, *Export Now.*
* Mona Pearl, *Grow Globally: Opportunities for Your Middle-Market Company around the World.*
* John Warrillow, *Built to Sell: Creating a Business That Can Thrive without You.*

Search engine choices (with 2014 ranking from www.ebizmba.com):

Logo	Search Engine	eBizMBA Rank	Monthly Visitors
Google	#1 Google	1	1,100,000,000
bing	#2 Bing	15	350,000,000
YAHOO!	#3 yahoo	18	300,000,000
Ask	#4 Ask	25	245,000,000
Aol.	#5 AOL Search	245	125,000,000
wow	#6 WOW	271	100,000,000
	#7 WebCrawler	511	65,000,000
mywebsearch	#8 MyWebSearch	545	60,000,000
	#9 Infospace	892	24,000,000
info	#10 Info.com	1,064	13,500,000

Figure 27: Search engine choices

Other great sources and resources include

* YouTube,
* Play Store,
* iPhone Store, and
* smartphone apps.

Chapter 2: Add Value

Site and document links change; these were all tested at the time of publication. We apologize if they don't work; use your search engine skills to relocate them.

Economic Information by Country

* Economic Intelligence Unit, Country Reports: www.eiu.com
* Financial Times, Country Reports
* host country organizations dedicated to foreign expansion
* host country chamber of commerce
* host country investment & development agencies
* International Monetary Fund: www.IMF.org
* Internet Resources for International Economics and Business: http://www.loc.gov/rr/business/intl/
* United Nations: http://unstats.un.org/unsd/default.htm
* US International Trade Commission / International Economic Review: http://usitc.gov/
* World Economic Forum: www.weforum.org
* World Competitiveness Yearbook
* World Bank's "Ease of Doing Business Rankings": www.worldbank.org
* your embassy or commercial officers in potential host countries

Unemployment Data

* www.principalglobalindicators.org
* https://www.cia.gov/library/publications/the-world-factbook/rankorder/2129rank.html

Chapter 3: De-Risk

Site and document links change; these were all tested at the time of publication. We apologize if they don't work; use your search engine skills to relocate them.

Political Situation

* G8 Information Center: http://www.g7.utoronto.ca

Import/Export Activity

* Export Start-Up Kit: http://www.tradecomplianceinstitute.org
* foreign trade: www.census.gov/foreign-trade/ and https://usatrade.census.gov/
* Global Trade Analysis Project: https://www.gtap.agecon.purdue.edu/
* industrial production, retail turnover & import/export data: www.principalglobalindicators.org
* International Trade Administration, US Department of Commerce: http://www.trade.gov/
* International Trade Compliance Institute website: http://www.tradecomplianceinstitute.org
* International Trade Data System: http://www.itds.gov/
* International Trade Desk: http://users.aol.com/tradedesk/trade.htm

* trade data & analysis: http://export.gov/tradedata/index.asp and www.census.gov/foreign-trade/www/sec4.html
* Trade Information Database: http://www.tradecomplianceinstitute.org
* US Foreign Trade Program: www.census.gov/foreign-trade/data/index.html
* US trade statistics by market & industry: www.trade.gov/mas/ian/tradestatistics/index.asp
* world trade links: trade reports, trade promotion and analysis, regulations, statistics: http://www.fita.org/
* World Trade Organization (WTO): http://www.wto.org (country-specific and world trade regulations)

Industry Analysts and Market Research (primarily fee-based services)

* Computer Review: www.computerreview.com
* Digital Clarity Group: www.digitalclaritygroup.com
* Forrester Research: www.forrester.com
* Gartner Group: www.gartner.com
* IBISWorld: www.ibisworld.com
* IDC (International Data Corporation): www.idc.com
* Informa Telecoms & Media: www.informatandm.com
* McKinsey & Company: www.mckinsey.com
* Ovum Ltd.: www.ovum.com
* SNL Kagan: www.snl.com
* Yankee Group: www.yankeegroup.com

Business Practices and Culture

* www.Kissbowshakehands.com
* www.executiveplanet.com

Time Zone Converters

* Smartphone clock will have a time zone converter
* www.timezoneconverter.com
* www.timeanddate.com/worldclock
* www.worldtimebuddy.com

Currency Converter and Exchange Rate Resources

* www.bloomberg.com/markets/currencies/currency-converter
* www.gocurrency.com
* www.google.com/finance/converter
* www.x-rates.com/calculator

Obtaining Cheap International Flights

* Airfare Watchdog: http://www.airfarewatchdog.com/
* airplane configurations: www.seatplans.com and http://www.seatguru.com/
* alerts when prices go down: www.yapta.com
* flight costs between different cities. http://www.airninja.com/

Travel Tips

* Forbes tips: http://www.forbes.com/sites/dorieclark/2012/06/07/5-tips-to-maximize-your-international-business-travel/
* Gadling tips: http://www.gadling.com/2012/09/17/10-tips-for-international-business-travel/
* Inc.com tips: http://www.inc.com/guides/201103/7-tips-for-foreign-business-travel.html

* Tech Republic tips, including eating right: http://www.techrepublic.com/blog/10-things/10-tips-for-coping-with-international-business-travel/#
* *USA Today*, navigating in a city when you don't know the language: http://traveltips.usatoday.com/navigate-foreign-city-dont-language-1676.html
* What and how to pack for a one-week trip: http://importexport.about.com/od/DoingBusinessIn/a/PackingForAnInternationalBusinessTrip.htm

Robert and Janet's Miscellaneous Travel Tips

* Don't rent a car until you have been to a country multiple times.
* Don't rent a car until you have been in-country for more than one day.
* Don't rent a car if you are only going to be in a city for 1–2 days; it's not worth it.
* If you are a runner or a walker, after you land somewhere, run or walk around the area of the hotel for 30, 45, or 60 minutes. Get acquainted with landmarks, shops, and public transportation.
* Always take the business card from the hotel with the hotel's address.
* Learn the basics of direction in the language of the country: left, right, straight. Language dictionary or Smartphone app work well for this.
* Travel safe, don't accept a room on the first floor, near the elevator, or near the stairs.

Share Your Travels, Record Your Experience, Personal Travel Guides

* smartphone apps like HipGeo and FourSquare
* smartphone app TagWhat

In-country Transportation

* find rides, smartphone app: Uber
* public transportation in a foreign city: http://blog.wehostels.com/public-transportation-foreign-country/
* subway smartphone app: AllSubway

Cell Phone and Internet Access

* ATT WiFi abroad: http://attwifiabroad.com/iosDevices/
* iPhone: http://www.idownloadblog.com/2009/04/23/tips-traveling-internationally-iphone/
* iPhone data: http://www.macworld.com/article/2057969/how-to-avoid-big-international-iphone-data-charges.html
* "Staying Connected While Abroad": http://www.transitionsabroad.com/listings/living/resources/stayingconnected.shtml

Primary Research: Survey and Data Collection Tools

* Google Consumer Surveys: www.google.com/consumersurveys
* Key Survey: www.keysurvey.com
* Survey Monkey: www.surveymonkey.com
* Zoomerang: www.zoomerang.com

Chapter 4: Find a Mountain Guide

Site and document links change from time to time; these were all tested at the time of publication. We apologize if they don't work; use your search engine skills to relocate them.

Government Resources for Help Finding a Mountain Guide

* Export.gov home page: http://www.export.gov/index.asp

Financial Information on Representative Companies, Partners, or Customers

* Dun & Bradstreet: http://www.dnb.com
* Tradenex: http://www.tradenex.com (region specific for Asia)

Mountain Guides(There are many; these are a few of our favorites mentioned in Built for Global)

* Daniel Turner Global
  * http://www.danielturner.global (global business development)
  * http://www.danielturner.pro (proposal/copy writing & presentation)
  * http://www.danielturner.today (economic journalism)
* Kimberly Benson, Zenaida Global
  * www.zenaidaglobal.com (transforming your international presence)

Other Helpful Sources and Resources

* Market Intelligence: https://www.export.gov/Market-Intelligence
* Foreign Traders Index (FTI): https://www.foreign-trade.com/index.htm
* Export.gov Gold Key Service: https://www.export.gov/search#/search?q=gold%20key%20service&_k=6rlm2p
* *Guidebook for US Services: The Export of the 21st Century* (World Trade Press Publications, tel.: 415-433-9084)

* International Company Profile (ICP) http://store.worldtradepress.com/Services_The_Export_the_21st_Century.php
* Trade Compass: http://www.trade-compass.com
* National Trade Data Bank (NTDB): http://www.trade.gov/mas/ian/tradestatistics/ and http://www.export.gov/tradedata/
* UNIDO (United Nations Industrial Development Organization): http://www.unido.org
* United Nations Statistics Division: http://www.un.org/Depts/unsd/
* USITC (US International Trade Commission): http://www.usitc.gov/

Chapter 5: Build Trust

Site and document links change from time to time; these were all tested at the time of publication. We apologize if they don't work; use your search engine skills to relocate them.

Communication Tools (There are many more than these, and new ones become available all the time)

* Google Hangout
* Skype
* Webex
* Smartphone communication tools
    * WhatsApp
    * Telegram

National Trade Show and Education Conference

* http://export.gov/

Raising Money

* http://www.tradeupfund.com

Trade Opportunities

* BR Trade (contact information, product codes, trade transportation, balance of trade for specific countries): http://www.brtrade.com/

Regional or Country-Specific Resources

* *Bolivia:* IBCE (International Trade Institute of Bolivia): http://ibce.org.bo/
* *Canada:* ExportSource: http://www.gov.mb.ca/trade/export/links/ex_exsrce.html
* *Canada:* http://www.canadabusiness.ca/eng/page/2839/
* *Canada:* Statistics Canada: http://www.statcan.ca/start.html
* *Caribbean:* Caribbean Export Development Agency: http://www.carib-export.com
* *China:* CETRA (China External Trade Development Council): http://www.taitra.org.tw/
* *China:* World Trade Database: http://www.wtdb.com/
* *Europe:* IBT Partners: http://ibtpartners.com/us
* *European Union:* http://www.europa.org
* *Germany*: GABA (German American Business Association): http://www.gaba-network.org/
* *Italy:* Institute for Statistics in Italy: www.istat.it
* *Japan:* Overseas Economic Cooperation Fund, Japan: http://www.jbic.go.jp/en

* *Latin America:* Inter-American Development Bank: http://www.iadb.org
* *Russia:* State Committee of the Russian Federation on Statistics (Goscomstat): http://www.gks.ru/
* *South Asia:* SAARC (South Asian Association of Regional Cooperation): http://www.saarcyellowpages.com
* *Spanish-speaking hemisphere, research, markets, events and experts:* The Americas Information Gateway System:
http://www.gmspmi.com/index.php?Content=RelatedWebsites
http://www.tradecorridors.org/
* *Taipei:* CETRA (China External Trade Development Council): http://www.taitra.org.tw/
* *Taiwan:* CETRA (China External Trade Development Council): http://www.taitra.org.tw/

Food & Agriculture

* FAO (Food & Agriculture Organization: http://www.fao.org
* Foreign Agricultural Service, US government: http://www.fas.usda.gov/

Appendix 2

Acronym Decoder Ring

Definitions come from *Wikipedia* (www.wikipedia.org), *Webster's International Dictionary*, and the crazy minds of Robert Pearlstein and Janet Gregory.

10k = The SEC (Securities and Exchange Commission) Form 10-K is a required annual report that gives a comprehensive summary of a company's financial performance. It contains more information than a company's glossy annual report. A Form 10-K is required for companies with more than $10 million in assets (among other conditions) and applies regardless of whether the securities are publicly or privately traded.

10Q = The SEC Form 10-Q is a quarterly report of financial performance required for all publicly traded corporations.

2X, 3X, 4X, "n" X = Two times, three times, four times, or *n* times. Multiplicative factor of *n* times some baseline amount

B2B = Business to business. A company that sells its products and services to other businesses.

B2C = Business to consumer. A company that sells its products and services directly to consumers.

B2G = Business to government. A company that sells its products and services to government (federal, state, or local), which will use them to support government-sponsored policies or programs.

B2P = Business to partner. A company that sells its products and services to or through partners, who will resell to business, consumers, or government.

BRIC = Brazil, Russia, India, and China. (BRICS adds South Africa.) These countries are often grouped together representing large growing economies that are a mix of advanced and developing.

CEO = Chief Executive Officer. The highest-ranking senior executive of a company. If he or she has operational responsibilities, the CEO will also carry the title of president.

CRM = Customer relationship management. Processes implemented to manage a company's interactions with customers and prospects. It is commonly used to describe software that manages these processes.

CV = Curriculum vitae. Profile of professional experience. A CV is typically longer and contains more information than a résumé, but they are used for the same purpose.

DIY = Do it yourself. Creating things for themselves without the aid of paid professional.

Expat = Expatriate (also commonly misspelled "ex-patriot"). A person temporarily or permanently residing in a country other than that of their citizenship. In business it refers to a professional or skilled worker sent abroad by a company with whom the person is employed.

F2F = Face-to-face. Meeting in person with another individual.

FUD = Fear, uncertainty, and doubt. Things that create worry, uncertainty, and apprehension, especially when entering into the unknown.

GDP = Gross domestic product. The market value of *all* officially recognized final (not raw) goods and services produced within a country in a year. It's an indicator of standard of living.

IP = Intellectual property. A legal term that refers to creations of the mind such as music, literature, discoveries, and inventions. Under intellectual property laws, owners of intellectual property are granted certain rights and protections via patent, copyright, trademark, design right, etc.

IPO = Initial public offering. A company offers shares to investors on the New York Stock Exchange or NASDAQ. Through this process a private company transforms into a public company, raising capital for expansion and to monetize the investments of early private investors.

IMF = International Monetary Fund. The International Monetary Fund is an international organization of 180+ countries working to foster global monetary cooperation, secure financial stability, facilitate international trade, and promote sustainable economic growth. www.imf.org

IT = Information technology. Depending upon use, the term can refer to an industry segment, infrastructure, or a department within a company responsible for a combination of computer equipment, software, and telecommunications.

ITA = International Trade Association. A division of the US Department of Commerce. www.ita.doc.gov/bems/index.htm

JV = Joint venture. A joint venture is a business agreement in which the parties agree to develop, for a specific time period, a new entity and new assets by contributing equity.

MAN = Money, authority, and need. Ability and willingness to buy.

MBA = Master of business administration. Higher education degree bestowed by a university for study in the scientific approach to business management.

MOU = Memorandum of understanding. Nonbinding agreement signed by two parties, usually between a prospective customer and a supplier.

N-A-B-C = Need, approach, benefits per cost, and competition. SRI International's formula for a value proposition introduced in the book *Innovation* by Carlson & Wilmot. A value proposition should include four components: 1) important customer or market need, 2) your approach to satisfy the need, 3) benefits per cost to the customer, and 4) competition or alternatives available.

NAICS = North American Industry Classification System. The standard for categories used by federal statistical agencies in classifying business in North America. www.naics.com

NASA = National Aeronautics and Space Administration. The US government agency responsible for the civilian space program along with aeronautics and aerospace research.

NTDB = National Trade Data Bank. A database compiled and run by the US federal government. The data bank contains information on US import-export, international investments, trade statistics, projections, exchange rates, and other information relating to international business and trade. www.stat-usa.gov

OA = Order administration. Department within a company responsible for processing orders placed by customers; responsible for sales orders, setting up new accounts, managing existing accounts, and seeing that orders are fulfilled by the company.

P&L = Profit and loss. A financial statement of a company showing revenues and expenses during a particular period.

PhD = Doctor of philosophy (Latin: *philosophiae doctor).* One of the highest postgraduate academic degrees awarded by universities.

PoC = Proof of concept. A pilot, trial, test or demonstration of feasibility and use. May be offered as money-back guarantee or contingent purchase.

RFI = Request for information. Customer-issued criteria to one or more vendors when seeking information to solve a problem. Similar to RFP, RFQ, or tender but usually does not ask for pricing.

RFP = Request for proposal. Customer-issued criteria to multiple vendors when seeking a solution to a problem. May also be referred to as RFQ or tender.

RFQ = Request for quotation. Customer-issued criteria to multiple vendors when seeking price comparison for similar offerings. May also be referred to as RFP or tender.

ROI = Return on Investment. The concept is to measure the impact of an investment made. The investment could be people, time, resources, or money. The impact is yield toward the accomplishment of some goal, such as saving money or making money. It's a means to compare investments and to measure the effectiveness of an investment.

SAP = Standard accounting practices. A set of rules that a company must follow when reporting information on its financial statement. Standard accounting practice guidelines allow companies to be compared to each other because they have followed the same rules. SAP in the United States is also referred to as GAAP, or generally accepted accounting principles.

SEC = Securities and Exchange Commission. Agency of the US government that is responsible for regulating and enforcing laws that affect the nation's securities, stocks, and options.

SME = Small to Medium Enterprise. Business whose personnel numbers fall below a specified limit.

TV = Television. Okay, that one was obvious!

US *or* **USA** = United States of America. Yes, you already knew that!

USD = US dollar. The currency of the United States. A single dollar is divided into one hundred cents, the monetary subunit.

VAR = Value-added reseller. A company that adds features or services to an existing product and then resells it as a more complete solution or integrated offering.

VP = Vice president. Organizational title (but you knew that!).

WTO = World Trade Organization. Membership organization of countries organized to address rules of trade between member countries. www.wto.org

Appendix 3

Fundamentals Worth Knowing

Anticipate basic personal and professional needs before leaving home to avoid the simple problems. When traveling to advanced countries, you will find life similar to the United States, with a fundamentally reliable infrastructure. On the other hand, travel to emerging and developing countries may present some challenges, especially when outside the country's capital city or major metropolitan centers. Infrastructure basics may be variable, unreliable, or even unavailable. Here are a few simple tips on infrastructure basics: time zones, proximity, in-country transportation, power converters, mobile access, and drinking water.

Time zones. Figuring out time-zone differentials can give you a brain cramp. The good news is that most smartphone clocks will do this for you, or you can find an app for time zone conversion. Robert and Janet also have one on their laptops to help arrange business meetings. If you have the luxury of picking a country or region based on personal preference, base it on your circadian rhythms. If you are a morning person living on the West Coast of the United States, pick countries in Europe and the Middle East. If you want to keep to a regular nine-to-five schedule, consider countries to the north and south in similar time zone bands, like Canada, Central America, or South America. If you are a night owl and prefer working at night, Asia, Australia, and China will fit your circadian rhythms. Time-zone conversion tools are plentiful; you will need one.

Proximity is both time and place. It's the joy of sitting for hours inside a metal tube called an airplane only to feel like a soggy pretzel on arrival. Robert flies coach class to stretch tight travel budgets. Robert's strategy to arrive ready for action is sit in an aisle seat and bring a sleeping pill, ear plugs, and eye shades. Janet prefers a window seat and melatonin, but the outcome is the same: get some sleep. You will also find that your body prefers one direction over the other. For Janet, traveling west works best for her body clock. Check which airlines fly in/out of country. Having more than one option helps avoid flight delays in the event of labor disputes or airline industry problems. Flights with only one connection will improve your chances of arriving in-country on the day and time you were expecting.

In-country transportation options. Think about the customers who will buy and use your product offering. You may need to transport product or people to service your customers. What are the in-country conveyance options via rail, air, sea, and road? Various factors will influence your transportation needs, including business requirements, type of goods, storage options, insurance, destination, cost, weight, and more. Often more than one mode of transportation will be used, which may raise questions of hand-off, storage, and security. Enlist the assistance of your mountain guide and your home team to explore these options. The goal is to balance quality, cost, organization, and time.

Power converters and transformers. Our dependence on electricity is unquestionable. We need to keep our toys up and operating. Business relies on electricity for both professional and personal needs; a successful business trip requires power for everything from computers and smartphones to shavers and hair dryers. What "wall wart" do you need? Do you need a plug adapter to change the configuration of prongs that stick into the wall? Or do you need a converter-transformer combo that both changes the prong configuration and does voltage or power conversion? Don't worry; you don't need to be an electronic genius. Check online or visit a local electronics store for some help; in our area that might be Best Buy or Radio Shack. It's good to avoid blowing the circuit breaker in your hotel room and melting your electronics. OOPS! If this is a last-minute detail you forgot to consider, the electronic shop at the international terminal will be very helpful, even if it is a bit more expensive.

Figure 28: Plug configurations

Mobile phone and Internet access. Reliable Internet access may be important to your travels and worth checking out in advance. We are addicted to our smartphones and laptops. Internet access provides the link to connect with your company and family back home. Internet access may be important to your product offering for operation, service, or reporting. Speed, bandwidth, availability, and reliability of Internet access are important to a wide range of industries, from high-tech products to agricultural equipment.

Check with your mobile carrier to get international services enabled before leaving the United States.

Drinking water. There is nothing worse than getting sick on a business trip. Waterborne bacteria are the easiest to avoid. Drink bottled water when you are in countries where water does not consistently meet quality levels expected by Westerners. In remote areas of early-emerging countries, protect yourself from waterborne bacteria by not opening your mouth in the shower and by brushing your teeth with bottled water. Stomach problems can bring an otherwise successful business trip to a screeching halt, and it's just not worth chancing it.

Appendix 4

Compensate and Motivate

There are many ways to compensate and motivate your mountain guide. The most common methods are:

* Commission
* Retainer
* Bonus
* Expense Reimbursement
* Other incentives

They can be used alone or, more commonly, in combination.

You probably don't need to be reminded … but compensation structure should be part of a time-bounded agreement; this allows for revision at the end of the specified time frame.

Commission

Commission is a variable compensation-plan element based on the achievement of specific financial goals, such as bookings, revenue, or payment received.

Commission is the most common compensation arrangement with a mountain guide. Robert always starts with commission as the primary compensation when in negotiation with a mountain guide. If possible Robert tries to negotiate a straight-commission plan. It is a simple, action-oriented approach to compensation because the representative gets paid a percentage of a sale. To avoid ambiguity, commission is further defined by order status such as booking, revenue, or payment received.

Commission on booking is when an order is received and terms are accepted by your company. Payment is made close to the transaction point when the representative has substantially completed his or her role. Your company carries the risk of cancellation, delivery, and collections. If there is a long lead time between booking and revenue recognition, it rewards the mountain guide for his or her achievement, but your company will not like the time gap.

Commission on revenue is when an accepted order has met the criteria of revenue recognition per standard accounting practices (SAP). For products this can occur when the product ships from point of origin, upon delivery, or upon installation, as defined by SAP or customer contract. For a service business, revenue recognition is typically on delivery or completion of services. Risk is shared by the mountain guide and your company; payment to the mountain guide is delayed until your company can recognize revenue.

Commission on payment is when your company has received cash or a financial instrument for the value of the order. Contractual arrangements with the customer may specify payment in advance, on delivery, or at specific milestones. Commission is paid to the representative on a pay-as-paid basis. The mountain guide carries more risk with payment delays and must rely on your company's timely ability to deliver products and collect payment.

The advantage of commission-based compensation is the results orientation. Mountain guides have incentive to sell as much as possible. The more they sell, the more they make. The disadvantage is that if they find your offering is harder to sell or has a longer sales cycle than other offerings they represent, they will likely lose interest and not put effort into selling your product.

Commission rates vary from country to country and the type of offering. Determining commission rate can be a bit complicated, and commission rates can be as low as 2 percent and as high at 25 percent. Robert and Janet have typically employed a 5 to 10 percent commission rate, factoring in retainer, overhead, and company profit margin.

Commission can also vary according to sales volume, which can be a motivator for the representative to sell more. For example, the representative may get 5 percent for sales up to $100,000 USD, 7 percent for $100,000 to $1 million USD, and 10 percent for everything over $1 million.

Treat your mountain guide fairly. Your mountain guide is not only a business contact in-country but also an extension of your company. The rate of business success in-country is a direct function of the representative you select.

Retainer

Fixed compensation paid in advance for specified work is a retainer. We will use the term "retainer" for convenience, but your company may refer to fixed compensation with some other terminology, like "guarantee," "allowance," "budget," or something else. A retainer signifies that your company is entering a mutual action-oriented agreement with the mountain guide. The specified work is typically outlined in a working agreement, as we outlined in "Establish Agreement."

Retainers are common for attorneys or accounting services in order to secure or keep their services available or "on call" as required. In a work-for-hire relationship, the retainer establishes mutual commitment between the mountain guide and your company, similar to the way a salary commits a full-time employee to work for a company. The retainer falls between a one-time contract and full-time employment.

If your company is a well-recognized brand name, a retainer may be unnecessary. Mountain guides will be proud to carry your company name on their business cards or in their business operations. Retainers can be strategic, especially if they prevent your mountain guide from working with a competitor. Robert has also worked with mountain guides on straight commission and then added a retainer later in the relationship for fear of losing the person's services when getting traction in-country took longer than expected.

It is important to specify the expected services to be performed for the retainer services. Janet always puts work expectations in writing and updates them periodically, either monthly, quarterly, or annually, at a minimum; the working agreement becomes a living document. Janet always maintains an action-oriented retainer; it keeps the mountain guide focused on performance and reduces the possibility of paying something for nothing. Set the expectation that the required services will change over time. Expectations for the mountain guide are the job description accompanied by management objectives and a working agreement.

Retainers can be a fixed negotiated rate or a variable hourly rate depending on the expectations, role, and management objectives. Both models are frequently used. A fixed negotiated rate works well when expecting a minimum level of commitment for autonomous activities that yield results. A variable hourly rate works well with more measureable, transactional activity expectations. Robert and Janet more commonly work on a fixed negotiated rate, which addresses their business needs.

Retainer rates vary depending on the country, expertise level of the representative, and work to be accomplished. The retainer rate is typically based on a 10 to 50 percent uplift on what a full-time employee would be paid if hired in-country. The higher the uplift, the more unique or difficult the task.

This means that it will require a bit of investigation or research to determine a fair fee.

Here's an example of how it works: if a full-time salary for an equivalent person in-country is $50,000 USD annually, when uplifted by 14% to account for benefits that would be $57,000 USD equivalent. If you expect the representative to spend 50 percent of the time working for you, the retainer rate would be $28,500 USD per year. If the mountain guide is paid monthly, divide the annual rate by twelve months to arrive at a $2,375 USD monthly retainer.

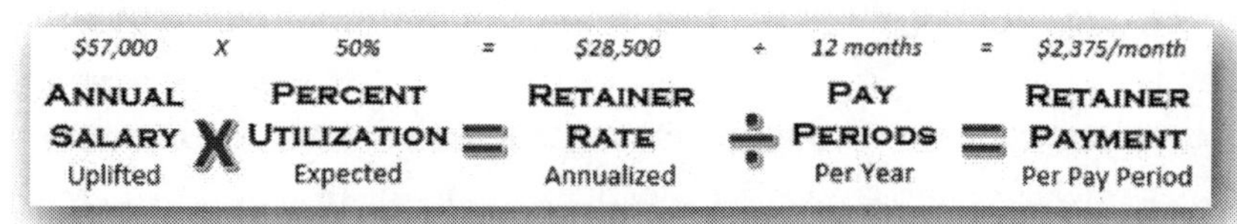

Figure 29: Method for retainer calculation

Obviously, all of the numbers in this example will change based on the country you are entering, the role the mountain guide will fill, the amount of time you will utilize services, and the number of pay periods. But, you get the idea of how it works.

A similar approach can be used when working with companies, although a company will typically have a predefined pricing approach for services. When working with companies as your mountain guide, this calculation method will help you to evaluate and negotiate relative value.

Bonuses

A bonus is often added to a retainer as a reward for good performance or achieving specific goals, such as setting up meetings, finding qualified leads, signed MOUs, or obtaining proof-of-concept customers.

Bonuses provide motivation for performance and achieving important milestones other than revenue generation. They can be defined within the compensation agreement or provided as a "surprise gift" for exceptional performance.

When engaging a mountain guide for tasks other than sales, bonuses are often employed as a compensation component. A bonus should be based on something measureable and specific, such as on-time completion or achievement above a base level of expectation. Tasks will be specific to your business, such as localization, retail displays, installation, training, or maintenance.

High-quality performance is often motivated or rewarded with a bonus. Quality can be a subjective measurement. We would recommend that bonuses for quality performance be based on measureable elements, such as customer satisfaction surveys or net promoter scores.

Exceptional service from a mountain guide over a period of time may be rewarded with an unexpected bonus as a thank-you for service. When a company transitions from launch to business operations within a country and the services of a loyal mountain guide may no longer needed, a termination bonus makes a nice thank-you. **Good mountain guides will work their way out of a job!**

The combined use of retainer plus bonus is common in the early stages of taking a company outside of the United States, because there are so many unknown factors. Bonuses are a form of variable compensation when international sales cycles are unknown and the value proposition for in-country customer has not been validated. Bonuses can be based on revenue-producing action as well as non-revenue-producing events. Robert and Janet have often paid bonuses to mountain guides for obtaining nonbinding MOUs (memorandum of understanding). MOUs are often an important component to initiating a business relationship in many countries and worthy of a bonus as a reward.

Bonus amounts vary by the type of performance expectation and will vary from country to country. Bonuses should be significant enough to stand out as an important element of the overall compensation package. Bonuses must also be kept reasonable so that they do not disproportionally compensate the representative as compared to what a full-time annual salaried employee in-country might be worth.

Expense Reimbursement

Expense reimbursement is repayment for agreed-upon and actual out-of-pocket expenses incurred while performing the job.

Agree in advance on acceptable out-of-pocket expenses that would qualify for reimbursement, if any. In some business relationships, there is no expense reimbursement; the mountain guide is expected to absorb expenses as part of the cost of doing business. In other business relationships, there will be an acceptable list of reimbursable expenses up to a maximum allowable. A periodic budget may be defined for expenses, or advance approval may be required. Expenses submitted for reimbursement should follow the same or similar process as used by employees in the United States, which will likely require receipts and justification (statement of purpose).

For most mountain guides, cell phone, Internet services, or office expenses are *not* reimbursed, and the mountain guide is expected to assume those costs as part of doing business. Travel and entertainment are typically reimbursable with specific parameters for what is acceptable, what is not, and what requires prior approval.

Other Incentives

Other incentives can excite and inspire action or greater effort; other incentives can be offered as a reward for increased productivity or high performance.

Gifts are a common incentive added to a compensation arrangement. The gift should be something valued by the mountain guide. Gifts vary widely in cost and type depending upon what is being rewarded and why. Personal items such as a watch, computer tablet, subscription, smartphone, jewelry, artwork, or other valued tangible articles are common gifts. Business gifts of training, conferences, or workshops are also highly valued.

Recognition among peers is an acknowledgement of status and merits. Recognition could be internal, within the company, for outstanding performance. External, public acknowledgement within a technical field, industry, or business function can also be highly prized. Recognition may be accompanied by some special status or classification that could be displayed on a business card, website, or in an office, such as a plaque or trophy or a status level such as "Gold Partner." Public acknowledgement can be accomplished via announcement, press release, tweet, published article, case study, Facebook posting, or speaking engagement at an event.

Awards take many forms. Robert and Janet have both found that travel awards can be a good motivator. It could be an all-expenses-paid trip to a desirable destination or to your company headquarters. The award travel can combine business with pleasure. Business content could be some combination of training, meeting with key company representatives, and convening with other high performers.

Appendix 5

Tasks for a Successful PoC

PoC Task 1: Set PoC Goals and Objectives

* What results do you need to achieve with the PoC customers?

    * Ensure that the product functions to meet customer expectation.
    * Verify implementation and operational requirements are met.
    * Quantify value specific to in-country customer needs.

* How will success of the PoC be measured?

    * by you and your company
    * by your mountain guide
    * by your PoC customers

* Set realistic expectations.

    * Time: how long to import and implement?
    * Resource requirements: manpower, expertise, infrastructure, etc.
    * Capital: investment, contingency, other.

PoC Task 2: Prepare for Customer Contact

* Determine target customers to contact (mountain guide's recommendations and network connections).

    * *Vertical:* Best-suited industry segments. Identify prospective customers by name and location.

    * *Contacts:* Best-suited functional roles to make contact with (by title).Make first contact with people who have the need and a pain point that your product can satisfy; if they are not decision-makers and buyers, they will introduce you to the right people.

    * *Channel Partners (if applicable):* Best-suited route to market (resellers, retailers), VARs (value-added resellers), distributors- or wholesalers). These partners fill the gap for delivery, implementation- and in-country support.

* Build presentations and useful sales tools.

    * product demonstration (if applicable).
    * collateral: website, data sheet & relevant case studies (from the United States)
    * sales materials: Elevator pitch, presentation, qualifying questions, objection handling, competitive matrix, etc.

* Establish roles of all parties involved in the PoC process.

    * What needs to be done? Lead generation, initial contact, sales process, proposal generation, agreement negotiation, closing, etc.
    * Who is responsible? Mountain guide, you, United States–based sales support, sales engineer, others as appropriate.

PoC Task 3: Go Sell Something!

* Create interest and qualify PoC prospect.

* Align influencers involved in the decision and PoC operation.

* Prepare PoC proposal.

* Negotiate agreement.

    * Key component of the agreement is to mutually establish success criteria.
    * How will you and the customer decide that the agreement/pilot/trial was successful?
    * What do you need to prove? Build the success criteria around what you need to prove. The product works. The product works in-country. The product works to address a specific customer need in-country.

PoC Task 4: Monitor PoC Delivery for Success

* Assure that post sales roles and responsibilities are well understood, both in-country and back in the United States. This should cover every detail from shipment to arrival to installation. Considerations for technical support and user support need to be assigned.

* Locally, the mountain guide will participate and monitor progress to ensure success criteria are met. The mountain guide can position the customer for a successful close, but remember, typically the mountain guide is not the closer. As required, also have an SE or customer-support representative assigned to assist in this important part of the process.

* The mountain guide will assist in obtaining permission from the customer to be a reference or for case study, testimonial, or other business endorsement. This commitment from the customer will require your direct involvement and maybe that of another company executive. Once permission is received from the customer, marketing should be ready to gather information for the case study.

* Determine who will have responsibility for final closure and conversion to purchase; it could be you, the mountain guide, or an in-country partner.

Appendix 6

Memorandum of Understanding (MOU)

A memorandum of understanding (MOU) is a statement of work or relationship between two or more parties. It is a more formal alternative to a "gentleman's agreement," in which two parties agree that a handshake confirms a deal.

Since this is about your company entering a new country, your company will be one of the parties. The other party or parties will typically be prospective customers, partners, or resellers. The mountain guide is your representative, so the mountain guide will typically *not* be a signing party unless the mountain guide is an organization with in-country authority that is important to the relationship outlined in the MOU.

MOUs are nonbinding agreements that state what the parties want to achieve at a relatively high level. An MOU will often precede the formal, legally binding agreement. It allows the parties to begin working toward their stated goals in good faith. Legal agreements overseas can take time to complete. Legal agreements include the "four corners" of law: offer, acceptance, consideration (such as money in exchange for products or services), and intention to be legally bound.

As we have already highlighted, MOUs are viewed as important in many countries. Depending upon the nature of the MOU, a signing event may be planned that includes local dignitaries and the press. The signing of an MOU is often accompanied by the issuance of a press release.

A Story over Coffee with Robert Pearlstein
Robert has many great stories to tell of different MOU signings. In one situation, an MOU was signed early in a relationship with a prospective Japanese value-added reseller (VAR). The MOU was an important sign of commitment, alignment, and mutual aspirations. Japan is a culture of consensus where many people need to review and agree on relationships.

The VAR organized a signing event with press coverage. The MOU was influential to the VAR's internal organizational support for the developing relationship. The MOU also provided a powerful catalyst for introduction to prospective customers. The result was a long and successful business relationship.

Illustrations and Tables

CHAPTER 2: ADD VALUE

CHAPTER 3: DE-RISK

CHAPTER 4: FIND A MOUNTAIN GUIDE

CHAPTER 5: BUILD TRUST

CHAPTER 6: ARE YOU GOING GLOBAL?

APPENDIX

Notes

Chapter 1: Going Global

1. TolpaTek is a fictitious company; its characters, and story represent an imaginary composite of Robert Pearlstein and Janet Gregory's business experiences.

2. Deborah Wince-Smith, National Summit on American Competitiveness, Chicago.

3. Frank Lavin and Peter Cohan, *Export Now: Five Keys to Entering New Markets* (John Wiley & Sons, 2011).

4. The NYC Experience: Queens, 2013.

5. Geoffrey A. Moore, *Crossing the Chasm* (Harper Business, 1991).

Chapter 2: Add Value

6. Ernesto Sirolli, narrator on NPR's TED Radio Hour, "Is There a Right and a Wrong Way to Help Someone," October 18, 2013.

7. Mona Pearl, *Grow Globally: Opportunities for Your Middle-Market Company around the World* (John Wiley & Sons, 2011).

8. Curtis Carlson and William Wilmot, *Innovation: The Five Disciplines for Creating What Customers Want* (Crown Business, 2006).

9. Michael E. Porter, *Competitive Advantage: Creating and Sustaining Superior Performance* (The Free Press: Simon & Schuster, 1998).

10. *Ibid.*

11. Pearl, *Grow Globally.*

12. J. Michael Gospe Jr., *The Marketing High Ground* (Word Press, 2011).

13. *Ibid.*

14. Classification blended from the UN, IMF, and World Economic Forum.

15. Gospe, *The Marketing High Ground.*

Chapter 3: De-Risk

16. Andrew Aitken "Andy" Rooney (1919-2011), American radio and television writer.

17. PR Newswire, news release, August 19, 2015, http://news.sys-con.com/node/3420509.

18. IMF World Economic Outlook (WEO), April 2015.

19. W. Chan Kim and Renée Mauborgne, *Blue Ocean Strategy: How to Create Uncontested Market Space and Make the Competition Irrelevant* (Harvard Business School Publishing, 2015).

20. *Wikipedia*, s.v. "Diversification," last modified April 20, 2017, https://en.wikipedia.org/wiki/Diversification (finance).

21. Ronald Inglehard and Miguel Basanez, *Changing Human Beliefs and Values: A Cross-Cultural Sourcebook Based on the World Values Surveys and European Values Studies* (2010).

22. World Values Map reprinted with permission from Dr. Ronald Inglehard.

23. World Bank and Quandl.

24. Brock Williams and J. Michael Donnelly, *U.S. International Trade: Trends and Forecasts* (Washington, DC: Congressional Research Service, 2012).

Chapter 4: Find A Mountain Guide

25. Pearl, *Grow Globally.*

26. Apple Insider http://appleinsider.com/articles/09/11/03/canalys_q3_2009_iphone_rim_taking_over_smartphone_market/

Chapter 5: Build Trust

27. Williams and Donnelly, "U.S. International Trade."

28. Original source unknown. Quote is attributed to many, including Ken Blanchard, modern management author; Douglas Englebart, inventor of the computer mouse; and Herodotus, ancient Greek historian.

29. Inspired by "Why People Do What They Do" by The Performance Technologies Group Pty. Ltd. (T/A PTG Global).

30. The concept of influencers and their characteristics was inspired by Target Account Selling.

31. Thomas J. Peters and Robert H. Waterman Jr., *In Search of Excellence* (Harper Business Essentials, 2006).

32. Turner Global can be found at www.danielturner.global (Global Business Development) and at www.danielturner.pro (International Proposals and Presentations).

33. Moore, *Crossing the Chasm.*

34. Robert B. Miller and Stephen E. Heiman, *Strategic Selling* (Warner Business Books, 2011).

35. Tom Hopkins, *Selling for Dummies* (John Wiley & Sons, 2015).

36. Neil Rackham, *SPIN Selling: Situation, Problem, Implication, and Need-Payoff* (McGraw-Hill Book Company, 1988).

37. Henry Blodget, "And Now Nokia Has a New Problem: It Might Go Bankrupt," *Business Insider*, April 19, 2012, http://www.businessinsider.com/nokia-bankrupt-2012-4.

38. Statista: The Statistics Portal, www.statista.com.

39. http://www.socialbakers.com/statistics/.

Chapter 6: Are You Going Global?

40. Not a scientific principal or theory. Described in several self-help and wellness programs.

41. Investopedia definition from www.investopedia.com.

42. Motley Fool Staff, "Why Should I Invest?" *The Motley Fool*, http://www.fool.com/investing/beginning/why-should-i-invest.aspx.

Index

Made in the USA
Lexington, KY
21 June 2017